KAREL THE ROBOT

KAREL THE ROBOT
A Gentle Introduction to the Art of Programming

Second Edition

Richard E. Pattis

Revision By:

Jim Roberts
School of Computer Science
Carnegie Mellon University

Mark Stehlik
School of Computer Science
Carnegie Mellon University

John Wiley & Sons, Inc.
New York ▪ Chichester ▪ Brisbane ▪ Toronto ▪ Singapore

Acquisitions Editor	Steven Elliot
Marketing Manager	Susan Elbe
Assistant Marketing Manager	Laura McGayhey
Senior Production Editor	Nancy Prinz
Designer	Lynn Rogan
Manufacturing Manager	Susan Stetzer

This book was set in 10/12 Times Roman by Publication Services and was printed and bound by Courier Stoughton. The cover was printed by Phoenix Color Corp.

Recognizing the importance of preserving what has been written, it is a policy of John Wiley & Sons, Inc. to have books of enduring value published in the United States printed on acid-free paper, and we exert our best efforts to that end.

Library of Congress Cataloging-in-Publication Data

Pattis, Richard E.
   Karel the robot : a gentle introduction to the art of programming
/ Richard E. Pattis.–2nd ed. / revision by Jim Roberts, Mark
Stehlik.
      p.   cm.
   Includes index.
   ISBN 0-471-59725-2
   1. Electronic digital computers–Programming.   I. Roberts, Jim
(Jim A.), 1946–   .   II. Stehlik, Mark.   III. Title.
QA76.6.P38   1995
005.1–dc20   94-8087
                                                       CIP

Printed in the United States of America

10 9 8 7 6 5 4 3 2 1

To the Pattises, Shaffers, and Olshanskys—REP

To Linda—JR

To my parents, Lillian and Ladislav, and to Sylvia—MS

PREFACE

The programming landscape has changed significantly since the initial publication of *Karel the Robot* in 1981. Today there are new programming languages, new programming *paradigms*, and new and more powerful computers. Even though Pascal no longer enjoys the popularity it did in the 1980s, Karel is still as vibrant and valid an introduction to the programming and problem-solving processes as it was when first introduced.

We believe that most people will not actually have to program a computer as part of their everyday lives, either now or in the future. However, many people will need to be able to use a computer and will occasionally need to do something with the machine beyond the "ordinary." Simply put, they will have to solve some type of computer problem. We solve various kinds of problems every day; problem solving is part of our lives. This book will introduce you to problem-solving approaches that can be used with computers. Unfortunately, some people believe programming requires a "different" way of thinking. We don't agree with this statement. Instead of changing the way you think, this book will change how you apply your problem-solving skills to different kinds of problems.

For the experienced student programmer, this edition should provide insights into the problem-solving and program design processes that will make the student an even better programmer. It will also improve understanding of computer science concepts such as loop invariants and recursion. For individuals who want to begin a thorough sequence of training and education in programming, computer science, or both, Karel provides a solid foundation on which to begin your work.

For novice programmers, this book will give some insight into the programming process from two distinctly different points of view: the planner's and the implementer's. All the problems can be thought about, discussed, and planned in English. Once you have developed your plan, the actual syntax of the robot programming language has very few rules to get in your way as you become the implementer or programmer.

For individuals who do not want to program but need to have a feel for the process, Karel is an excellent tool for providing that insight.

Supplements. An instructor's manual is also available for the text that contains a detailed description of the changes from the first edition; numerous pedagogical suggestions for teaching the material based on many years of using Karel in introductory programming courses at the college level; and solutions to all the in-text exercises.

Software to simulate Karel is available on IBM PCs, Apple Macs, and a variety of "mainframes." The PC/Mac software can be directly purchased from John Wiley & Sons (accompanying copies of this book). Site licenses for all machines can be obtained by contacting:

Richard E. Pattis
2823 Broadway Avenue E.
Seattle, WA 98102

March 1994

Jim Roberts
Mark Stehlik

ACKNOWLEDGMENTS

This edition could never have existed without the first edition, so it is clearly appropriate to acknowledge the creative genius of Richard Pattis and the ground-breaking manuscript that is the first edition of *Karel the Robot*. It is always easier to modify wheels rather than reinvent them, and it is even easier when the wheel with which you are starting is almost perfectly circular.

Ideas are never formed in a vacuum, and we would like to acknowledge the Intro Programming Group at Carnegie Mellon University for providing a positive torr environment in which to test out ideas, see which ones work, and run with those that do. There are many individual people who help make an idea into a book. First and foremost, the authors would like to thank Steven Elliot, acquisitions editor at John Wiley, for believing in this project and getting it started. The authors would like to express their appreciation to the following people who reviewed all versions of the second edition manuscript: Roland Untch, Clemson University; Joe Kmoch, Washington High School, Milwaukee, Wisconsin; Billibon Yoshimi, Columbia University; Peter Henderson, SUNY/Stony Brook; Georgette Geotsi, University of Bridgeport; Tim Thurman, University of Kansas; and Peter Casey, Central Oregon Community College. We also acknowledge the help provided by Maria Fischer in getting everything out the door on time.

We also thank the following people who provided feedback on the first version of the manuscript and helped point us in the right direction: Phyllis Sturman; Douglas Grannes; Terry Brink, Lock Haven University of Pennsylvania; and Gordon Bugby, University of Pittsburgh.

Thanks also to Linda and Syl.

JR
MS

I want to take this opportunity to thank Jim Roberts and Mark Stehlik for writing the second edition of *Karel the Robot*. As long-time teachers and experimenters with *Karel,* they have brought to this book many fresh ideas, new insights, and interesting examples and problems.

I also want to thank Phil Miller, for being a tireless promoter (and amplifier) of the ideas embodied in *Karel*; Douglas B. Stein, for translating the Karel Simulator to run on PCs; and Steven Elliot, for having the persistence and clout to ensure the second edition was published.

I attribute the lengthy success of the first edition to a seminal idea (thanks to Seymour Papert) and the excellent feedback I received while translating this idea into a book. For their invaluable comments, I remain indebted to Marsha Berger, Jim Boyce, Denny Brown, Michael Clancy, Kalen Delaney, Tom Dietterich, Joseph Faletti, Bob Filman, John Gilbert, Brent Hailpern, Wayne Harvey, Mike Kenniston, Jock Mackinlay, Keith L. Phillips, Mark Tuttle, and David Wall.

Finally, I want to thank my original editor, Gene Davenport, and the staff at Wiley who helped me create a book that was successful enough to spawn a second edition: Elaine Rauschal, Loretta Saracino, and Rosemary Wellner.

REP

CONTENTS

1 THE ROBOT WORLD

This chapter introduces Karel[1] the robot and sketches the world it inhabits. In later chapters, where a greater depth of understanding is necessary, we will amplify this preliminary discussion.

1.1 KAREL'S WORLD

Karel lives in a world that is unexciting by present-day standards (there are no volcanoes, Chinese restaurants, or symphony orchestras), but it does include enough variety to allow the robot to perform simply stated, yet interesting, tasks. Informally, the world is a grid of streets that Karel can traverse. It also contains special objects that Karel can sense and manipulate.

Figure 1–1 is a map illustrating the structure of Karel's world, whose shape is a great flat plane with the standard north, south, east, and west compass points. This world is bounded on its west side by an infinitely long vertical wall extending northward. To the south, it is bounded by an infinitely long horizontal wall extending eastward. These boundary walls are made from solid *neutronium*, an impenetrable metal that restrains Karel from falling over the edge of the world.

Crisscrossing the world are horizontal streets (running east–west) and vertical avenues (running north–south) at regular, one-block intervals. To help you distinguish between streets and avenues, remember that the A in Avenue points north and the V in aVenue points south. A corner, sometimes referred to as a street corner or an intersection, is located wherever a street and an avenue intersect. Karel can be positioned on any corner, facing one of the four compass points. Both streets and avenues are numbered; consequently, each corner is uniquely

---

[1]Karel is named after Czechoslovakian dramatist Karel Čapek, who popularized the word "robot" in his play R.U.R. (Rossum's Universal Robots). The word "robot" was derived from the Czech word "robota," meaning forced labor.

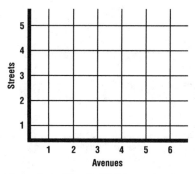

Figure 1–1 Karel's World

identified by its street and avenue numbers. The corner where 1st Street and 1st Avenue intersect is named the origin. The absolute location of the origin is the intersection of 1st Street and 1st Avenue. The origin also has a relative location; it is the most southwesterly corner in Karel's world. We will use both absolute and relative locations to describe the position of Karel and objects in Karel's world.

Besides Karel, there can be two other types of objects in the world. The first type is a wall section. Wall sections are also fabricated from the impenetrable metal neutronium, and they can be manufactured in any desired length and pattern. They are positioned between adjacent street corners, effectively blocking

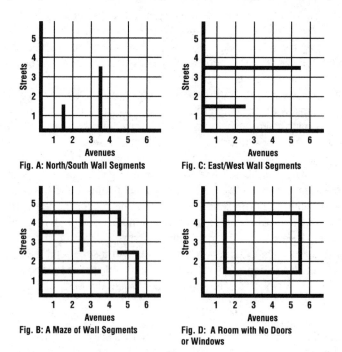

Fig. A: North/South Wall Segments

Fig. C: East/West Wall Segments

Fig. B: A Maze of Wall Segments

Fig. D: A Room with No Doors or Windows

Figure 1–2 Different Wall Segment Arrangements in Karel's World

Karel's direct path from one corner to the next. Wall sections are used to represent obstacles around which Karel must navigate such as hurdles and mountains. Enclosed rooms, mazes, and other barriers can also be constructed from wall sections. Figure 1–2 shows some typical wall arrangements Karel might find in the world.

The second type of object in Karel's world is a beeper. Beepers are small plastic cones that emit a quiet beeping noise. They are situated on street corners and can be picked up, carried, and put down by Karel. Some of Karel's tasks involve picking up or putting down beepers arranged in patterns or finding and transporting beepers. Figure 1–3 shows one possible beeper arrangement.

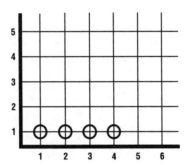

Figure 1–3   One Pattern of Beepers in Karel's World

1.2   KAREL'S CAPABILITIES

We now shift our attention away from Karel's world and concentrate on Karel itself. Karel is a mobile robot; it can move forward in the direction it is facing, and it can turn in place. Karel can also perceive its immediate surroundings using rudimentary senses of sight, sound, direction, and touch.

Karel sees by using any one of three television cameras that point straight ahead, to the left, and to the right. These three cameras are focused to detect walls exactly half a block away from Karel. Karel also has the ability to hear a beeper, but only if the beeper is on the same corner as the robot. (The beepers beep quietly.) By consulting an internal compass, Karel can determine which direction is being faced. Finally, Karel is equipped with a mechanical arm that can be used to pick up and put down beepers. To carry these beepers, Karel wears a soundproof beeper-bag around its waist. Karel can also determine if it is carrying any beepers in this bag by probing the bag with the mechanical arm.

Whenever we want Karel to accomplish a task in the world, we must supply a detailed set of instructions that explains how to perform the task. Karel is able to read and follow such a set of instructions, which is called a program.

What language do we use to program (here we use "program" to mean "write instructions for") Karel? Instead of programming Karel in English, a natural language for us, we write the program in a special <u>programming language</u>, which was designed to be useful for writing robot programs. Karel's robot programming language has a vocabulary, punctuation marks, and rules of grammar. This language is simple enough for Karel to understand; yet it is powerful and concise enough to allow us to write brief and unambiguous programs for Karel.

1.3   TASKS AND SITUATIONS

A <u>task</u> is just something that we want Karel to do. The following examples are tasks for Karel: move to the corner of 15th Street and 10th Avenue, run a hurdle race (with wall sections representing hurdles), escape from an enclosed room that has a door, find a beeper and deposit it on the origin, and escape from a maze.

A <u>situation</u> is an exact description of what Karel's world looks like. Besides the basic structure of Karel's world, which is always present, wall sections and beepers can be added. To specify a situation completely, we must state the following information.

- What is Karel's current position? We must specify both Karel's location (in absolute or relative terms) and what direction it is facing.
- What is the location and size of each wall section in the world?
- What is the location of each beeper in the world? This information includes specifying the number of beepers in Karel's beeper-bag.

We specify situations in this book by a small map or a brief written description. If we know the number of beepers that Karel has in the beeper-bag, then the maps in Figure 1–4 completely specify different situations. The <u>initial situation</u> for any task is defined to be the situation in which Karel is placed at the start of the task. The <u>final situation</u> is the situation that Karel is in when it turns itself off. Unless told otherwise, you may assume that Karel starts all tasks with an empty beeper-bag.

Figure 1–4 shows six initial situations that are typical for tasks that Karel will accomplish in the coming chapters.

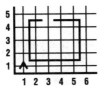

Fig. A: A Room Has 1 Door. Karel is at the origin and facing north. Karel must enter the room.

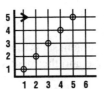

Fig. B: A Diagonal Line of Beepers. Karel is facing east. Karel must pick all beepers.

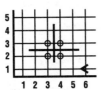

Fig. C: A "+" Wall Arrangement with Beepers. From Karel's starting position, it must pick the four beepers.

Fig. D: Karel must escape the maze.

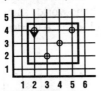

Fig. E: Beepers are scattered randomly in a box. Karel is facing south in the northwest corner of the box. Karel must pick all of the beepers in the box.

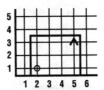

Fig. F: A Box with a Beeper. Karel is facing north in the northeast corner of the box. Karel must find the beeper.

Figure 1–4 Six Different Tasks for Karel to Perform

1.4   PROBLEM SET

The purpose of this problem set is to make sure that you have a good understanding of Karel's universe and the robot's capabilities before moving on to a robot program.

1. Which of the following directions can Karel face?

   northeast
   east
   south–southwest
   north
   164 degrees
   vertical
   down

2. What "objects" other than Karel can be found in Karel's world?
3. Which of the "objects" listed in (2) can Karel manipulate or change?
4. What "reference points" can be used in Karel's world to describe Karel's exact location in the world?
5. Give the "exact" location of Karel in the worlds shown in Figure 1–5. Also give the "relative" location of Karel in these worlds.

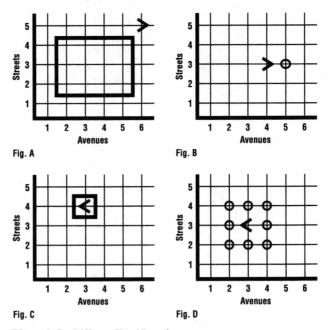

Figure 1–5   Different Karel Locations

2 PRIMITIVE INSTRUCTIONS AND SIMPLE PROGRAMS

This chapter begins our study of Karel's programming language. We will start with a detailed explanation of the five primitive instructions that are built into Karel's vocabulary: **move**, **turnleft**, **pickbeeper**, **putbeeper**, and **turnoff**. Using these instructions, we can command Karel to move through the world and handle beepers. Section 2.4 demonstrates a complete robot program and discusses the elementary punctuation and grammar rules of Karel's programming language. By the end of this chapter, we will be able to write programs that instruct Karel to perform simple obstacle avoidance and beeper transportation tasks.

Before explaining Karel's primitive instructions, we first must define the technical term *execute*: Karel executes an instruction by performing its associated action. Karel executes a program by carrying out the instructions in the program.

2.1 CHANGING POSITION

Karel understands two primitive instructions that change its position. The first of these instructions is **move**, which changes Karel's location.

> **move** When Karel executes a **move** instruction, it moves forward one block; it continues to face the same direction. To avoid damage, Karel will not move forward if it sees a wall section or boundary wall between its current location and the corner to which it would move. Instead, Karel turns itself off. This action, called an *error shutoff*, will be explained further in Section 2.5.

From this definition, we see that Karel executes a **move** instruction by moving forward to the next corner. However, Karel performs an error shutoff when its front is blocked. Both situations are illustrated in the next figure. Figure 2–1 shows the successful execution of a **move** instruction. The wall section is more than half a block away and cannot block Karel's move.

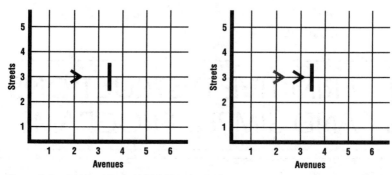

Figure 2–1   (*a*) Karel in the Initial Situation Before a **move** Instruction. (*b*) Karel in the Final Situation After Executing a **move** Instruction.

In contrast, Figure 2–2 shows an incorrect attempt to move. When Karel tries to execute a **move** instruction in this situation, it sees a wall section. Relying on its self-preservation instinct, Karel performs an error shutoff.

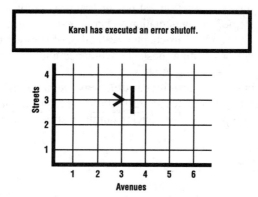

Figure 2–2   The Result of Karel Attempting to Move When Its Front Is Blocked Is an Error Shutoff.

The second primitive instruction that changes Karel's position is **turnleft**. This instruction changes the direction that Karel is facing but does not alter its location.

turnleft   Karel executes a **turnleft** instruction by pivoting 90° to the left. Karel remains on the same street corner while executing a **turnleft** instruction. Because it is impossible for a wall section to block Karel's turn, **turnleft** cannot cause an error shutoff.

Karel always starts a task on some corner, facing either north, south, east, or west. Karel cannot travel fractions of a block or turn at other than 90° angles.

Although **move** and **turnleft** change Karel's position, after executing either of these instructions, Karel still is on some corner and still is facing one of the four compass points.

Karel's designer purposely did not provide a built-in **turnright** instruction. Would adding a **turnright** to Karel's list of primitive instructions allow the robot to perform any task it cannot accomplish without one? A moment's thought—and the right flash of insight—shows that the **turnright** instruction is unnecessary; it does not permit Karel to accomplish any new tasks. The key observation for verifying this conclusion is that Karel can manage the equivalent of a **turnright** instruction by executing three **turnleft** instructions.

2.2 HANDLING BEEPERS

Karel understands two primitive instructions that permit it to handle beepers. These two instructions perform opposite actions.

pickbeeper   When Karel executes a **pickbeeper** instruction, it picks up a beeper from the corner on which it is standing and then deposits the beeper in the beeper-bag. If a **pickbeeper** instruction is attempted on a beeperless corner, Karel performs an error shutoff. On a corner with more than one beeper Karel picks up one, and only one, of the beepers and then places it in the beeper-bag.

putbeeper   Karel executes a **putbeeper** instruction by extracting a beeper from the beeper-bag and placing it on the current street corner. If Karel tries to execute a **putbeeper** instruction with an empty beeper-bag, an error shutoff is performed.

Beepers are so small that Karel can move right by them; only wall sections and boundary walls can block its movement.

2.3 FINISHING A TASK

Finally, we need a way to tell Karel that its task is finished. The **turnoff** instruction fulfills this requirement.

turnoff   When Karel executes a **turnoff** instruction, it turns off and is incapable of executing any more instructions until it is restarted on another task. The last instruction in every robot program must be a **turnoff** instruction.

2.4   A COMPLETE PROGRAM

In this section we provide a task for Karel and a complete program that instructs the robot to perform the task. The task, illustrated in Figure 2–3, is to transport the beeper from 2nd Street and 4th Avenue to 4th Street and 5th Avenue. After Karel has put down the beeper, it must move one block farther north before turning off.

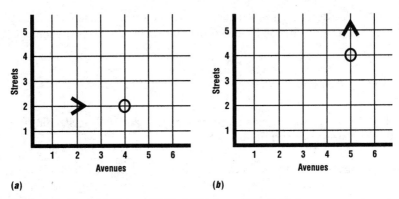

Figure 2–3   The (*a*) Initial and (*b*) Final Situations of Karel's Task

The following program instructs Karel to perform this task. The program uses the five primitive instructions, a few new words from Karel's vocabulary, and the semicolon (";") punctuation mark. First, we will discuss Karel's execution of this program, and then we will analyze the general structure of all robot programs.

```
BEGINNING-OF-PROGRAM
  BEGINNING-OF-EXECUTION
    move;
    move;
    pickbeeper;
    move;
    turnleft;
    move;
    move;
    putbeeper;
    move;
    turnoff
  END-OF-EXECUTION
END-OF-PROGRAM
```

We must note that this is just one of many sequences of instructions that will correctly perform the stated task.

2.4.1 Executing a Program

Before Karel can execute a program, the robot first reads it to make sure it has no errors. We will discuss errors later; for now we will assume that our program is correct.

How does Karel execute a program? Karel executes a program by sequentially carrying out each instruction between the words BEGINNING-OF-EXECUTION and END-OF-EXECUTION. This is done without omitting any instructions in a strict top-to-bottom order. Karel continues executing instructions until it either executes a turnoff instruction or performs an error shutoff.

Of course, Karel is not a real robot, so it cannot read a program or execute it. To determine what a program does, we simulate or trace Karel's execution of it. Simulating or tracing a robot program means that we must systematically execute the program exactly as Karel would, recording every action that takes place. We can *simulate* a robot program by using markers on a sheet of paper (representing Karel and its situation). We *trace* a robot program by following the sequence of instructions in the order Karel executes them. The ability to simulate Karel's behavior quickly and accurately is an important skill that we must acquire. Let's follow a simulation of our program. In the following simulation, 2,2 means 2nd Street and 2nd Avenue.

```
BEGINNING-OF-PROGRAM
   BEGINNING-OF-EXECUTION
```
	Karel is at corner 2,2 facing east, with 0 beepers in the beeper-bag.
move;	Karel moves east to 2,3.
move;	Karel moves east to 2,4.
pickbeeper;	Karel picks 1 beeper; 1 beeper in bag.
move;	Karel moves east to 2,5.
turnleft;	Karel remains on 2,5, faces north.
move;	Karel moves north to 3,5.
move;	Karel moves north to 4,5.
putbeeper;	Karel puts 1 beeper down; 0 beepers in bag.
move;	Karel moves north to 5,5.
turnoff	Karel remains on 5,5 facing north and shuts off.

```
   END-OF-EXECUTION
END-OF-PROGRAM
```

Karel is done, and we have verified that our program is correct through simulation by tracing the execution of the program.

2.4.2 The Form of Robot Programs

Now that we have seen how Karel executes a program, let's explore the grammar rules of the robot programming language. Karel pays strict attention to grammar and punctuation rules, so our time carefully studying these rules is well spent. We start by dividing the symbols that Karel understands into three classes. The first class is punctuation marks, and its only member is the semicolon. All other symbols in Karel's vocabulary are classified as either instructions, examples of which we have already seen, or reserved words.

Reserved words are used to structure and organize the primitive instructions in Karel's language. To make the reading of programs easier, we show reserved words in upper-case letters and instructions in lower-case letters. This distinction should help us keep these two word classes separate. Note, however, that this is only for our benefit because Karel does not differentiate between upper-case and lower-case spelling of words.

In the following discussion, we explain the four reserved words and the punctuation rules used in this programming example. Before proceeding, let's review our program.

```
BEGINNING-OF-PROGRAM
   BEGINNING-OF-EXECUTION
      move;
      move;
      pickbeeper;
      move;
      turnleft;
      move;
      move;
      putbeeper;
      move;
      turnoff
   END-OF-EXECUTION
END-OF-PROGRAM
```

Every robot program must start with the reserved word **BEGINNING-OF-PROGRAM**. This word is followed by the reserved word **BEGINNING-OF-EXECUTION**,[1] which in turn is followed by a sequence of instructions. After this instruction sequence comes the reserved word **END-OF-EXECUTION**, finally followed by the reserved word **END-OF-PROGRAM**. Matching pairs of **BEGIN/END** reserved words are called delimiters, because they mark the beginning and end of some important entity.

The reserved word **BEGINNING-OF-EXECUTION** tells Karel where in the program to start executing instructions. The reserved word **END-OF-EXECUTION** does not tell Karel that it is finished executing a program; the **turnoff** instruction is used for this purpose. Instead, the reserved word **END-OF-EXECUTION**

---

[1] **BEGINNING-OF-EXECUTION** does not always directly follow **BEGINNING-OF-PROGRAM**. In the next chapter we will learn what can be placed between these two reserved words.

marks the end of the instructions that Karel will execute. If Karel is executing a program and reaches **END-OF-EXECUTION**, it means that a **turnoff** instruction has been omitted from the program, and Karel will report an error.

Now let's closely examine the semicolon punctuation of this program. The semicolon (";") serves to separate consecutive instructions. The rule we must follow is, "Each *instruction* is separated from the next *instruction* by a semicolon." We write each semicolon directly after the first of the two separated instructions. This simple punctuation rule is often misinterpreted as, "Each instruction is followed by a semicolon." The difference between these two punctuation rules can be detected by inspecting the **turnoff** instruction in the program. The **turnoff** instruction does not have a semicolon after it because it is followed by **END-OF-EXECUTION**, which is a reserved word, not another instruction. There is no rule requiring that reserved words be separated from instructions by semicolons. Notice that the "semicolon after each instruction" rule fails to punctuate this case correctly, but the "semicolon between instructions" rule succeeds. Also notice that two consecutive reserved words such as **BEGINNING-OF-PROGRAM** and **BEGINNING-OF-EXECUTION** are not separated by a semicolon.

This punctuation strategy is analogous to the way we write a set of numbers in mathematics. For example, we write the set consisting of the elements 1, 4, and 7 as {1,4,7}. In our analogy, the braces are delimiters, the numbers are instructions, and the commas between numbers take the places of semicolons. If we wrote this set as {1,4,7,} it would look as if we had forgotten to write the final number in the set. Similarly, if we included a semicolon after turnoff, Karel would expect to find another instruction, not the **END-OF-EXECUTION** reserved word. We must punctuate our programs carefully because many grammatical errors are the result of incorrect semicolon punctuation.

Finally, observe that the entire program is nicely indented. It is well organized and easy to read. As with our use of upper- and lower-case letters, this style of indenting is only for our benefit. Karel ignores the indentation of our programs just as it ignores the case of the letters we use to spell the words. The following program is just as easily read by Karel as the previous program.

```
beginning-of-program beginning-of-execution move; move;
pickbeeper; move; turnleft; move; move; putbeeper; move;
turnoff end-of-execution end-of-program
```

As this example illustrates, the importance of adopting a programming style that is easy to read by humans cannot be overemphasized.

2.5 ERROR SHUTOFFS

When Karel is prevented from successfully completing the action associated with a primitive instruction, it turns itself off. This action is known as an error shutoff, and the effect is equivalent to Karel's executing a **turnoff** instruction. But turning off is not the only way such a problem could be addressed. An alternative strategy could have Karel just ignore any instruction that cannot be executed successfully. Using this strategy, Karel could continue executing the program as if it had never been required to execute the unsuccessful instruction.

To justify the choice of executing an error shutoff, consider the following: once an unexpected situation arises—one that prevents successful execution of an instruction—Karel probably will be unable to make further progress toward accomplishing the task. Continuing to execute a program under these circumstances will lead to an even greater discrepancy between what the programmer had intended for Karel to do and what Karel is actually doing. Consequently, the best strategy is to have Karel turn off as soon as the first inconsistency appears.

So far, we have seen three instructions that can cause error shutoffs: **move**, **pickbeeper**, and **putbeeper**. We must construct our programs carefully and ensure that the following conditions are always satisfied.

- Karel executes a **move** instruction only when the path is clear to the next corner immediately in front of Karel.
- Karel executes a **pickbeeper** instruction only when it is on the same corner as at least one beeper.
- Karel executes a **putbeeper** instruction only when the beeper-bag is not empty.

These conditions are easily met if, before writing our program, we know the exact initial situation in which Karel will be placed.

The absence of a **turnoff** instruction in our program also results in Karel reporting an error. To avoid this possibility, we must remember to include a **turnoff** instruction as the last instruction in our program.

2.6 PROGRAMMING ERRORS

In this section we classify all programming errors into four broad categories: lexical, syntactic, execution, and intent. These categories are discussed using an analogy that helps clarify the nature of each error type. You might ask, "Why spend so much time talking about errors when they should never occur?" The answer to this question is that programming requires an inhuman amount of precision, and although errors should not occur *in principle* they occur excessively *in practice*. Therefore, we must become adept at quickly finding and fixing errors by simulating our programs.

A lexical error occurs whenever Karel reads a word that is not in its vocabulary. As an analogy, suppose that we are standing on a street in San Francisco and we are asked by a lost motorist, "How can I get to Portland, Oregon?" If we tell the motorist, "fsdt jkhpy hqngrpz fgssj sgr ghhgh grmplhms," we will have committed a lexical error. The motorist is unable to follow our instructions because it is impossible to decipher the words of which the instructions are composed. Similarly, Karel must understand each word in a program that it is asked to execute.

Here is a robot program with some lexical errors:

```
BEGINNING  OF PROGRAM          missing hyphens
    GEBINNING -OF-EXECUTION    misspelled word—order of
                                   letters and an extra space
        move;
        mvoe;                  misspelled word
        pick;                  unknown word
        move;
        turnright;             unknown word
        move;
        . . .
```

Even if Karel recognizes every word in a program, the program still might harbor a <u>syntactic error</u>. This type of error occurs whenever we use incorrect grammar or incorrect punctuation. Going back to our lost motorist, we might reply, "for keep hundred just miles going eight." Although the motorist recognizes each of these words individually, we have combined them in a senseless, convoluted manner. According to the rules of English grammar, the parts of speech are not in their correct positions. (We discussed the grammar rules for basic robot programs in Section 2.4.2.)

The following program contains no lexical errors, but it does have syntactic errors.

```
BEGINNING-OF-EXECUTION         Grammar Error—this should be the
                                   second line of the program
    BEGINNING-OF-PROGRAM       Grammar Error—this should be the
                                   first line of the program
        move;
        move;
        pickbeeper;
        move;
        turnleft               Punctuation Error—missing ";"
        move;
        move;
        putbeeper;
        END-OF-EXECUTION       Grammar Error—this is out of place
        move;
        turnoff
END-OF-PROGRAM
```

If our program contains either lexical or syntactic errors, Karel will discover them when it reads our program. In both cases, Karel has no conception of *what we meant to say*; therefore, it does not try to correct our errors. Instead, it informs us of the detected errors, and then it turns off because Karel is incapable of executing a program that it does not fully understand. This action is not an error shutoff, for in this case Karel never begins to execute the program. While discussing the next two categories of errors, we will assume that Karel finds no lexical or syntactic errors in our program and begins to execute the program.

The third error category is called an execution error. As with lexical and syntactic errors, Karel can also detect these errors when they occur. Execution errors occur whenever Karel is unable to execute an instruction successfully and is forced to perform an error shutoff. Returning to our motorist, who is trying to drive from San Francisco to Portland, we might say, "Just keep going for eight hundred miles." But if the motorist happens to be facing west at the time and takes our directions literally, the Pacific Ocean will be reached after traveling only a few miles. At this point, the motorist will halt, realizing that our instructions cannot be followed to completion.

Similarly, Karel turns off if asked to execute a primitive instruction that it cannot execute successfully. Instructing Karel to **move** when the front is blocked, to **pickbeeper** on a corner that has no beeper, and to **putbeeper** when the beeper-bag is empty are examples of execution errors, and each one results in an error shutoff.

The final error class is the most insidious, because Karel cannot detect this type of error when it occurs. We label this category of error an intent error. An intent error occurs whenever Karel successfully completes the program but does not successfully complete the task. Suppose our motorist is facing south when we say, "Just keep going for eight hundred miles." Even though these instructions can be successfully followed to completion, the motorist will end up somewhere in Mexico.

Here is an example of an intent error in a robot program: Karel is to pick up the beeper, move it one block to the north, put the beeper down, move one more block to the north, and turn off. (See Figure 2–4.)

```
BEGINNING-OF-PROGRAM
    BEGINNING-OF-EXECUTION
        move;
        pickbeeper;
        move;
        turnleft;
        putbeeper;
        move;
        turnoff
    END-OF-EXECUTION
END-OF-PROGRAM
```

There are no lexical, syntactic, or execution errors in this program. As far as Karel is concerned, when the turnoff is executed, everything is perfect. However, look at the task and look at the program. What is the error? The task is to move the beeper one block to the north, yet Karel moved the beeper one block to the east. The intent was a northerly move, but the final result was an easterly move. The

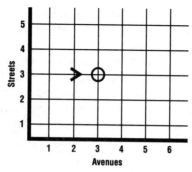

Figure 2–4   Karel's Initial Situation

program does not satisfy the requirements of the stated task and thus contains an error of intent.

Remember that Karel does not *understand* the task for which we have programmed it. All that Karel can do is execute the instructions we have written in our program. Thus, there is no way for Karel to know that the program did not accomplish what we intended.

Frequently, intent errors occur early in a program and later lead to execution errors. Once Karel makes a wrong turn or moves incorrectly, it is usually just a matter of time before the robot tries to move through a wall or pick up a beeper that is not where it should be. Just because an error shutoff occurs, it does not mean that the instruction being executed is wrong. A previous instruction could cause an error that does not manifest itself until much later in the execution of the program. In such cases, we must trace backward through the program from the instruction that caused the error shutoff, to discover which instruction started Karel on the errant path. This type of interaction between intent and execution errors is illustrated concretely in Problem 2.7–1.

2.6.1   Bugs and Debugging

In programming jargon, all types of errors are known as bugs. There are many apocryphal stories about the origin of this term. In one story the term "bug" is said to have been originated by telephone company engineers. They used the term to describe the source of random noises transmitted by their electronic communications circuits, saying that there were bugs in the circuits.

Another story originated with the Harvard Mark I Computer and Admiral Grace Murray Hopper.[2] The Mark I computer was producing incorrect answers, and when engineers took it apart, trying to locate the problem, they found that a

---

[2]You will find much information about Admiral Hopper and the Harvard Mark I computer in your library.

dead moth caught between the contacts of a relay was causing the malfunction—ergo, the first computer bug. Other stories abound, so perhaps we will never know the true "entomology" of this word.

The term "bug" became popular in programming to save the egos of programmers who could not admit that their programs were full of errors. Instead, they preferred to say that their programs had bugs in them. Actually, the metaphor is apt; bugs are hard to find, and although a located bug is frequently easy to fix, it is difficult to ensure that all bugs have been found and removed from a program. Debugging is the name that programmers give to the activity of removing errors from a program.

2.7 PROBLEM SET

The purpose of this problem set is to test your knowledge of the form and content of simple robot programs. The programs you are required to write are long, but not complicated. Concentrate on writing grammatically correct, pleasingly styled programs. Refer back to the program and discussion in Section 2.4 for rules and examples of correct grammar and punctuation. Verify that each program is correct by simulating Karel in the appropriate initial situation.

1. Start Karel in the initial situation illustrated in Figure 2–5 and simulate the execution of the program below. Karel's task is to find the beeper, pick it up, and then turn itself off. Draw a map of the final situation, stating whether an error occurs. If an execution or intent error does occur, explain how you would correct the program. This program has no lexical or syntactic errors.

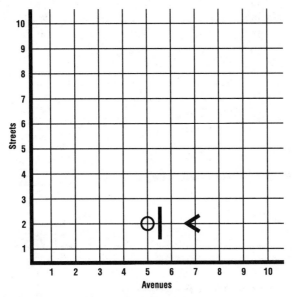

Figure 2–5   Initial Situation for Problem 1

```
BEGINNING-OF-PROGRAM
  BEGINNING-OF-EXECUTION
    move;
    turnleft;
    turnleft;
    move;
    turnleft;
    move;
    turnleft;
    move;
    pickbeeper;
    turnoff
  END-OF-EXECUTION
END-OF-PROGRAM
```

2. Carefully inspect the following program and correct all lexical and syntactic errors. *Hint*: There are eight errors—five errors involve semicolons, one is grammatical, and the other two errors are lexical. Confirm that each word is in an appropriate place and that it is a correctly spelled instruction name or reserved word. You may use the program in Problem 2.7–1 as a model for a lexically and syntactically correct program.

```
BEGINNING-OF-EXECUTION;
  BEGINNING-OF-PROGRAM
    move;
    move
    pickbeeper;
    move;;
    turnleft;
    move;
    move;
    turnright;
    putbeeper;
    move;
    turnoff;
  END-OF-EXECUTON
END-OF-PROGRAM;
```

3. What is the smallest, lexically and syntactically correct Karel program?
4. In most cities and towns we can "walk around the block" by repeating the following actions four times:
    * Walk to the nearest intersection.
    * Turn either right or left (the same one each time).
    If done correctly, we will return to our original starting place. Program Karel to "walk around the block." (See Figure 2–6.)

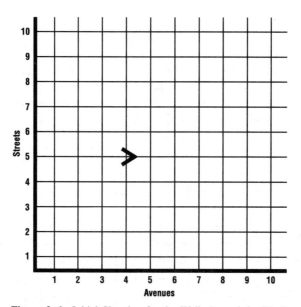

Figure 2–6 Initial Situation for the Walk Around the Block Task

5. Every morning Karel is awakened in bed when the newspaper, repre- sented by a beeper, is thrown on the front porch of the house. Program Karel to retrieve the paper and bring it back to bed. The initial situation is given in Figure 2–7, and the final situation must have Karel back in bed (same corner, same direction) with the newspaper.

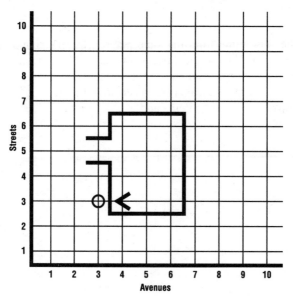

Figure 2–7 Initial Situation for the Newspaper Retrieval Task

6.   The wall sections in Figure 2–8 represent a mountain (north is up). Program Karel to climb the mountain and then plant a flag, represented by a beeper, on the summit; Karel then must descend the other side of the mountain. Assume that Karel starts with the flag-beeper in the beeper-bag. Remember that Karel is not a super-robot who can leap to the top of the mountain, plant the flag, and then jump down in a single bound. As illustrated, Karel must closely follow the mountain's face on the way up and down.

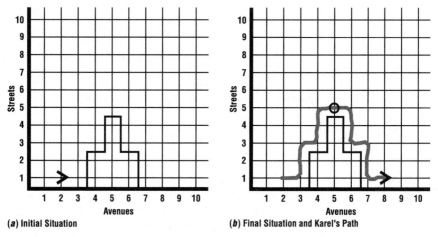

(*a*) Initial Situation   (*b*) Final Situation and Karel's Path

Figure 2–8   The Mountain-Climbing Task

7.   On the way home from the supermarket, Karel's shopping bag ripped slightly at the bottom, leaking a few expensive items. These groceries are represented by—you guessed it—beepers. The initial situation, when Karel discovered the leak, is represented in Figure 2–9. Program Karel to pick up all the dropped items and then return to the starting position.

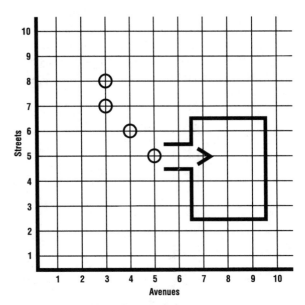

Figure 2–9 Initial Situation for the Grocery Pickup Task

8. Write a program that instructs Karel to rearrange the beeper pattern as shown in Figure 2–10.

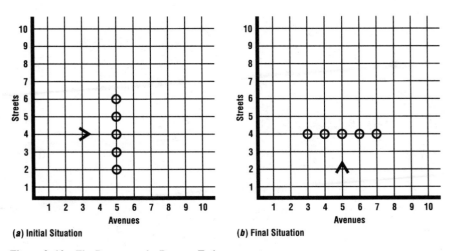

(*a*) Initial Situation   (*b*) Final Situation

Figure 2–10 The Rearrange the Beepers Task

9. Karel is practicing for the Robot Olympics. One of Karel's events is the shuttle race. The shuttle race requires Karel to move around two beepers in a figure 8 pattern (Figure 2–11). Write a program that instructs Karel to walk this pattern as fast as possible. (Fast implies as few instructions as possible.) Karel must stop in the same place it starts and must be facing the same direction.

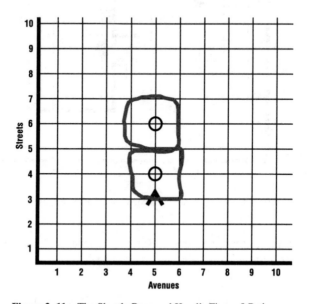

Figure 2–11   The Shuttle Race and Karel's Figure 8 Path

3 EXTENDING KAREL'S VOCABULARY

This chapter explains the mechanics of adding new instructions to Karel's vocabulary, block structuring, and several methods for planning, implementing, and testing our programs. The ability to extend Karel's vocabulary combined with these techniques can simplify our work in writing robot programs.

3.1 CREATING A MORE NATURAL PROGRAMMING LANGUAGE

In Section 2.1 we saw that Karel can perform the equivalent of a **turnright** instruction by executing a sequence of three **turnleft** instructions. However, writing three **turnleft** instructions for the simple act of turning right is both unnatural and verbose. It would be useful if Karel's programming language contained a more concise way of conveying these instructions.

Let's look at another clumsy aspect of robot programming. Suppose that we need to program Karel to travel over vast distances. For example, assume that the robot must move east ten miles (a mile is eight blocks long), pick up a beeper, and then move another ten miles north. Because Karel understands about moving *blocks* but not *miles*, we must translate our solution into instructions that move Karel one block at a time. This restriction forces us to supply a program that contains 160 **move** instructions. Although the conversion from miles to blocks is straightforward, it results in a very long and cumbersome program.

The crux of both these problems is that we think in one language but must program Karel in another. Rather than make programmers the slaves of the machine, continually forced to translate their powerful ideas into Karel's primitive instructions, Karel's designer turned the tables and endowed Karel with a simple mechanism to *learn* the definitions of new instructions.

Karel's learning ability is actually quite limited. Our programs can furnish the robot with a *dictionary* of useful instruction names and their definitions, but each definition must be built from simpler instructions that Karel already understands. By providing Karel with instructions that perform complex actions, we can build a vocabulary to correspond more closely to our own. Given this mechanism, we can solve our programming problems using whatever instructions are natural to our way of thinking, and then we can provide Karel with the definitions of these instructions.

Returning to our first example, we can inform Karel that the definition of a **turnright** instruction is three **turnleft** instructions. Similarly, we can define a **move-mile** instruction as eight **move** instructions. When Karel must execute either of these new instructions in a program, the robot looks up the definition associated with the instruction name and executes it. Now our unwieldy beeper-moving program can be written with a **move-mile** definition, containing eight **move** instructions and another 20 **move-mile** instructions. This program, containing 28 instructions, would be quite an improvement over the original program, which needed 160 instructions to accomplish the task.

Even though both programs move Karel exactly the same distance, the smaller program is much easier to read and understand. In complicated problems, the ability to extend Karel's vocabulary makes the difference between understandable and unintelligible programs. We will detail this extremely important definition mechanism in the next two sections.

3.2 A MECHANISM THAT DEFINES NEW INSTRUCTIONS

This section introduces the first component that is needed to define new instructions. Karel's definition mechanism defines a new instruction to have the same meaning as one other instruction. Yes, the learning mechanism is that simple; we can define a new instruction by using only one other instruction that Karel already understands. Concentrate on the details of this trivial definition mechanism for now, and in the next section we will discover how to increase its power dramatically. Isolated from a program, the general form of the definition mechanism is given below.

```
DEFINE-NEW-INSTRUCTION <new-name> AS
    <instruction>
```

This mechanism uses the reserved words **DEFINE-NEW-INSTRUCTION** and **AS**. The **DEFINE-NEW-INSTRUCTION** signals Karel that a new instruction is being defined, and **AS** separates the new instruction name from its definition. When this mechanism is used in a program, we replace <**new-name**>[1] by any word consisting of lower-case letters, numbers, and the hyphen ("-"). This word cannot be the name of an existing instruction or a reserved word. Despite the restrictions,

---

[1]We use the bracket notations (<**new-name**> and <**instruction**>) to help describe Karel's language in general terms. The bracketed word is a placeholder and must be replaced with the indicated component. For example, we may replace the bracketed word <**instruction**> by a **move** in one instance and by a **turnleft** in another. Appendix A contains a complete list of bracketed words and the associated words in Karel's vocabulary by which they can be replaced.

Karel's language does allow hyphenated names when a multiple-word name is needed (for example, `face-north` and `go-to-wall`).

We can replace <`instruction`> by any single instruction that Karel understands; this instruction becomes the definition of <`new-name`>. Possible replacements include all of the primitive instructions and any new instructions previously defined by using **DEFINE-NEW-INSTRUCTION**. Karel executes a new instruction by looking up its definition and performing the associated action.

The restriction of replacing <`instruction`> by a single instruction is extremely severe, and it will be rectified in the next section. However, even this simple form of **DEFINE-NEW-INSTRUCTION** can be useful. If Karel were ever sent to France, the French programmers might employ **DEFINE-NEW-INSTRUCTION** to create the following simple translations.

```
DEFINE-NEW-INSTRUCTION avance AS
move
```

and

```
DEFINE-NEW-INSTRUCTION tourne-a-gauche AS
turnleft
```

3.3   BLOCK STRUCTURING

When building complex commands such as `turnright` and `move-mile`, we frequently need to replace <`instruction`> by more than just one instruction. Karel's designer chose block structuring as the method to perform this replacement. Block structuring is simple enough for Karel to understand, and it is general enough to be used with other complex instructions in the robot programming language. Block structuring is accomplished by placing a sequence of instructions between the reserved words **BEGIN** and **END**, making one big instruction out of a sequence of smaller ones. We write a **BEGIN/END** block in the following way, using indentation to reinforce the idea that a **BEGIN/END** block represents one large, collective instruction.

```
BEGIN
  <instruction>;
  <instruction>;
  <instruction>;
       .              .
       .              .
       .              .
  <instruction>;
  <instruction>
END
```

Let's explore the properties of this new grammar rule in greater detail.

- The reserved words **BEGIN** and **END** delimit a block that consists of a sequence of instructions separated by semicolons. The internal punctuation of a **BEGIN/END** block is the same as the internal punctuation of the **BEGINNING-OF-EXECUTION/END-OF-EXECUTION** block. Remember that a semicolon does not separate the last instruction in the sequence from the reserved word **END**.

- We can write any number of instructions within a **BEGIN/END** block, and if we want, we may have only one. Although a single instruction does not need to be enclosed in a **BEGIN/END** block, this does not violate any of Karel's grammar rules.

- Karel executes a **BEGIN/END** block by sequentially executing the instructions within the block. Once Karel starts to execute a **BEGIN/END** block, all the instructions inside the block are eventually executed, unless a **turnoff** instruction is executed or an error shutoff occurs.

The fundamental property of a **BEGIN/END** block is that Karel understands the entire block to represent one instruction. This property permits us to replace <**instruction**> by a **BEGIN/END** block. Armed with the concept of block structuring, we can now completely solve the **turnright** problem by defining the following new instruction.

```
DEFINE-NEW-INSTRUCTION turnright AS
BEGIN
  turnleft;
  turnleft;
  turnleft
END;
```

So far, we have shown new instruction definitions only outside of a program. In Section 3.5, we show a complete program that uses the instruction definition mechanism. First, however, we must discuss the boundaries of Karel's understanding of new instructions.

3.4 THE MEANING AND CORRECTNESS OF NEW INSTRUCTIONS

Karel is a machine, a robot, a device completely devoid of intelligence. This is something that robot programmers must never forget. Karel does not "understand" what we "mean" when we write a program. It does exactly what we "say"—there is no room for interpretation. In Karel's world, just because we define a new instruction named **turnright**, it doesn't necessarily mean that the instruction really turns Karel to the right. For example, there is nothing that prevents using the following instruction definition.

```
DEFINE-NEW-INSTRUCTION turnright AS
BEGIN
  turnleft;
  turnleft
END;
```

According to Karel's rules of grammar, this definition is perfectly legal, for it contains neither lexical nor syntactic errors. But by defining **turnright** in this way, we tell Karel that executing a **turnright** instruction is equivalent to executing two **turnleft** instructions. Karel does not *understand* what a **turnright** instruction is supposed to accomplish; its only conception of a **turnright** instruction is the definition we provide. Consequently, any new instruction we define may contain an intent error, as this example demonstrates.

Besides intent errors, a new instruction can cause execution errors if it is defined by using primitive instructions that can cause error shutoffs. Can this incorrect definition of **turnright** ever cause an error shutoff? The answer is no, because **turnleft** instructions are immune to error shutoffs. As a result, it is impossible for Karel to detect that anything is wrong with this instruction.

This example is somewhat trivial because the error is obvious. With a more complex defined instruction, we must take care to write a definition that really accomplishes what its name implies. The name specifies *what* the instruction is intended to do, and the definition specifies *how* the instruction does what the name implies. The two must match exactly; otherwise, one or both must be changed.

When simulating Karel's execution of a defined instruction, we must adhere to the rule that Karel uses to execute these instructions—Karel executes a defined instruction by performing the actions associated with its definition. Do not try to shortcut this process by doing what the instruction *means* because Karel does not know what a defined instruction means; Karel knows only how it is defined. We must recognize the significance of this distinction and learn to interpret Karel's programs as literally as the robot does.

3.5 DEFINING NEW INSTRUCTIONS IN A PROGRAM

In this section we display a complete robot program that uses the instruction definition mechanism. We will first trace the execution of the program. (Recall that tracing is just simulating the execution of the instructions in the order that Karel does.) We will then discuss the general form of programs that use the new instruction definition mechanism. Karel's task is shown in Figure 3–1: it must pick up each beeper in the world while climbing the stairs. Following this figure is a program that correctly instructs Karel to accomplish the task.

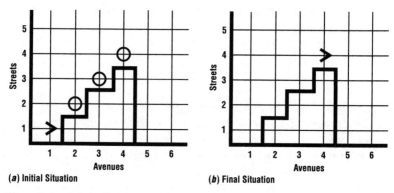

(a) Initial Situation   (b) Final Situation

Figure 3–1   A Stair-Cleaning Task for Karel to Perform

```
BEGINNING-OF-PROGRAM
  DEFINE-NEW-INSTRUCTION turnright AS    to here from
                                         #4, #13, or #22
  BEGIN
    turnleft;       #5        #14          #23
    turnleft;       #6        #15          #24
    turnleft        #7        #16          #25
  END;         return to #4  return to #13  return to #22


  DEFINE-NEW-INSTRUCTION climb-stair AS   to here from
                                          #1, #10, or #19
  BEGIN
    turnleft;       #2        #11          #20
    move;           #3        #12          #21
    turnright;      #4        #13          #22
    move            #8        #17          #26
  END;         return to #1  return to #10  return to #19


BEGINNING-OF-EXECUTION
  climb-stair;      #1
  pickbeeper;       #9
  climb-stair;      #10
  pickbeeper;       #18
  climb-stair;      #19
  pickbeeper;       #27
  turnoff           #28
END-OF-EXECUTION
END-OF-PROGRAM
```

To verify that this program is correct, we trace Karel's execution of it, carefully simulating the execution of the instructions. When Karel starts to execute a program, its focus is initially on the first instruction within the **BEGINNING-OF-EXECUTION/END-OF-EXECUTION** block. All the new instruction entries in Karel's dictionary are ignored for now. (When reading a book, we need only to look in the dictionary when we encounter a word whose definition we do not know.)

In the following sample program, Karel's initial focus is the **climb-stair** instruction, which is annotated as **#1**. Because the list of primitive instructions does not include **climb-stair**, the robot now consults its list of dictionary entries, looking for the definition of **climb-stair**. Karel's focus in the program temporarily leaves the **BEGINNING-OF-EXECUTION/END-OF-EXECUTION** block (Karel is very careful to remember where it was when it shifts its focus) and goes to the definition of **climb-stair** in the dictionary entry list. In the sample program, Karel's new focus is annotated as "to here from **#1**."

Karel focuses on the **BEGIN/END** block of the instruction, **climb-stair**, and encounters a **turnleft** (marked as **#2**). Karel executes the **turnleft** and now focuses on **#3**, **move**. Karel executes this **move** and focuses on **#4**, **turnright**. Since this instruction is not in the list of primitive instructions, Karel must again consult its list of dictionary entries, looking for the definition of **turnright**. Its focus shifts to the definition of **turnright**, which is marked as "to here from **#4**." Karel focuses on the **BEGIN/END** block and executes the three **turnlefts** marked **#5**, **#6**, **#7**. The execution of **turnleft** marked **#7** completes the execution of the instruction **turnright**. Its focus returns to the place in the program where it was previously (the **turnright** marked as **#4**), and execution continues with the following **move** instruction marked **#8**. After Karel performs this **move**, it is finished executing the instruction **climb-stair**. Therefore, its focus returns to the place in the program marked **#1** and it performs the **pickbeeper** that is marked **#9**. Karel repeats this same sequence of steps a second time for the **climb-stair** instruction marked **#10** and the **pickbeeper** that follows and again for the third **climb-stair** and **pickbeeper** instructions. Karel finally executes the **turnoff** instruction, and the program's execution is complete.

Notice that an instruction definition can become Karel's focus from any place in the program that uses that instruction. Karel always remembers the place in the program where it was when the definition of a new instruction is looked up. This allows the robot to return to its correct place and continue executing the program.

It is important for us to understand that no complex rules are needed to execute a program containing new instructions. Tracing Karel's execution of this program was a bit tedious, because each step is small and simple, but Karel is not equipped to understand anything more complicated. Karel is able to follow a very simple set of rules that tell it how to execute a program. Yet we can use these simple rules, coupled with Karel's willingness to follow them, to command the robot to perform nontrivial tasks.

We should now understand how Karel executes a program that includes the instruction definition mechanism. Next, we turn our attention to program form, and we make the following observations about the stair-cleaning program.

- In Chapter 2 we briefly mentioned that something could be written between the **BEGINNING-OF-PROGRAM** and **BEGINNING-OF-EXECUTION** reserved words. In our programming example, we saw that the definitions of the two new instructions are placed here. We must always write our new instruction definitions in this area. We call this portion of the program Karel's dictionary, and each definition a dictionary entry.

- The order of instruction definition is important: each instruction must be defined before it is used in either a subsequent definition or the **BEGINNING-OF-EXECUTION/END-OF-EXECUTION** block. In the example we just traced the **turnright** instruction must be defined first because **turnright** is used in the definition of **climb-stair**. Whenever this order is violated, Karel reports a lexical error.

- Now on to matters of punctuation, where we introduce two new semicolon punctuation rules. First, dictionary entries must be separated from one another by a semicolon. Second, the semicolon separating the last dictionary entry from the **BEGINNING-OF-EXECUTION/END-OF-EXECUTION** block is also necessary.

Karel's dictionary entries are not permanent, and Karel does not remember any definitions from program to program. Each time we write a robot program, we must include a complete set of all dictionary entries required in that program.

3.6 BOXING: HOW KAREL UNDERSTANDS A PROGRAM

In this section we explain how Karel can understand a program by isolating its constituents. The next section and subsequent chapters will demonstrate how we can use this information to help us recognize and avoid common pitfalls when writing and simulating programs. Specifically, in the next section we will show how Karel can detect a syntactic error (a missing **BEGIN/END** block in the definition of a new instruction) in a robot program.

We start our study of *boxing* by defining a unit to be either (1) a primitive or defined instruction name; (2) any type of **BEGIN/END** block; or (3) a complete dictionary entry. This third type of unit includes the reserved words **DEFINE-NEW-INSTRUCTION** and **AS**, the new instruction's name (which is already within its own box according to rule 1), and the instruction's definition (which is the first instruction following the **AS** and is also already in its own box). In the program shown in the accompanying illustration, taken from the previous section, we have drawn boxes around every unit. We call such an operation boxing. By boxing the programs, Karel is able to check for syntactic errors and determine exactly how to execute our programs.

Carefully study the following example to understand how boxing works. To help illustrate the process, the units have been numbered in the order Karel boxes them.

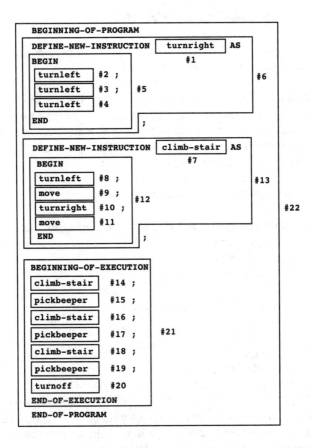

Karel starts boxing a program at its beginning. Generally, Karel builds units in a top-to-bottom order—but a unit cannot be boxed until all of its constituents have been boxed. For example, Karel cannot box a **BEGIN/END** block until all instructions within the **BEGIN/END** block have been boxed. Numerically, each box contains only boxes with smaller numbers. Therefore, within this top-to-bottom order Karel boxes primitive instructions first and then works outward, building larger units out of smaller ones.

The main geometric property of boxing is that boxes are either nested (one inside another) or adjacent (one following another). As a rule, units can never overlap. In addition, notice that the entire program is itself one big unit. Furthermore, semicolons are placed between every pair of adjacent units. This simple punctuation rule is a more uniform restatement of all the semicolon punctuation rules we have learned in our previous discussions of syntax. We will continue our analysis of Karel's grammar by using boxing.

3.7   AN UNGRAMMATICAL PROGRAM

Before reading this section, quickly look at the small program in the example below, and see if you can find a syntactic error.

This example illustrates the common programming mistake of omitting a **BEGIN/END** block. The program is nicely indented, but the indentation is misleading. The **DEFINE-NEW-INSTRUCTION** appears to define `turnright` correctly, but we have omitted the **BEGIN/END** block that should enclose the three `turnleft` instructions. Did you spot the mistake? It is not easy, because the indentation makes it look correct to us.

```
BEGINNING-OF-PROGRAM

    DEFINE-NEW-INSTRUCTION turnright AS
      turnleft;
      turnleft;
      turnleft

    BEGINNING-OF-EXECUTION
      move;
      turnright;
      turnoff
    END-OF-EXECUTION
END-OF-PROGRAM
```

While reading a program, Karel continuously checks it for lexical and syntactic errors. Karel discovers syntactic errors by boxing the program and checking for proper grammar and punctuation. In the following example, we illustrate how Karel finds the mistake in our program using boxing. Remember that the robot only reads the program's words and is unaware of our indentation and use of capital and lower-case letters.

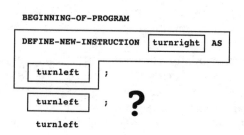

Karel successfully boxes the first unit, `turnright`, which is the new instruction name. Then it boxes the primitive instruction `turnleft` that directly follows the reserved word **AS**. By our omission of a **BEGIN/END** block, Karel now believes that the definition of `turnright` is completely boxed. Karel also believes that this definition is a single `turnleft` instruction. Karel next boxes the entire dictionary entry, notes the required semicolon, and continues. Then it boxes the next unit, which by the grammar rules must be another definition or the **BEGINNING-OF-EXECUTION/END-OF-EXECUTION** block. But here Karel finds an inconsistency; this next unit is a `turnleft` instruction, which does not satisfy either of Karel's options, so the robot tells us that a syntactic error has occurred. In summary, forgetting to use a necessary **BEGIN/END** block can lead to syntactic errors.

We are rapidly becoming experts at analyzing programs. Given a robot program, we should now be able to detect grammar and punctuation errors quickly. We should also be able to simulate programs efficiently. However, the other side of the programming coin, constructing programs, may still seem a little bit magical. The next section is a first step toward demystifying this process.

3.8 TOOLS FOR DESIGNING AND WRITING KAREL PROGRAMS

Designing solutions for problems and writing robot programs involve problem solving. One model[2] describes problem solving as a process that has four activities: definition of the problem, planning the solution, implementing the plan, and analyzing the solution.

The initial definition of the problem is presented when we are provided figures of the initial and final situations. Once we examine these situations and understand what task Karel must perform, we begin to plan, implement, and analyze a solution. This section examines techniques for planning, implementing, and analyzing robot programs. By combining these techniques with Karel's new instruction mechanism, we can develop solutions in an English-like manner that are easy to read and understand.

As we develop and write programs that solve Karel problems, these three guidelines must be followed:

- Our programs must be easy to read and understand.

- Our programs must be easy to debug.

- Our programs must be easy to modify in order to solve variations of the original task.

---

[2]G. Polya, *How to Solve It* (Princeton, N.J.: Princeton University Press, 1945, 1973).

3.8.1 Stepwise Refinement—A Technique for Planning, Implementing, and Analyzing Robot Programs

In this section, we discuss stepwise refinement, a method we can use to construct robot programs. This method addresses the problem of how we can naturally write concise programs that are correct, simple to read, and easy to understand.

It may appear natural to define all the new dictionary entries that Karel will need for a task first and then write the program using these instructions. But how can we know which new instructions are needed before we write the program? Stepwise refinement tells us first to write the program using any instruction names we desire, and then to write the definitions of these instructions. That is, first we write the sequence of instructions in the **BEGINNING-OF-EXECUTION/END-OF-EXECUTION** block, and then we write the definitions of the new instruction names used within this block. Finally, we assemble all of these separate pieces into a complete program.

We will explore this process more concretely by writing a program for the task shown in Figure 3–2. These situations represent a harvesting task that requires Karel to pick up a rectangular field of beepers.

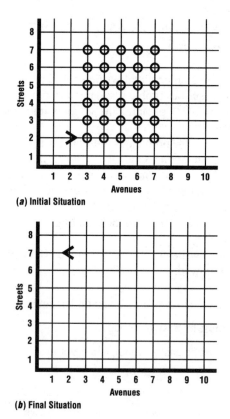

(a) Initial Situation

(b) Final Situation

Figure 3–2 The Harvest Task

3.8.1.1 The First Step—An Overall Plan

Our first step is to develop an overall *plan* to guide us in writing a robot program that allows Karel to perform the task. Planning is probably best done as a group activity. Sharing ideas in a group allows members to present different plans that can be thoughtfully examined for strengths and weaknesses. Even if we are working alone, we can think in a question and answer pattern such as the following.

Question: How can Karel pick a row?

Answer: Karel could move west to east across the southernmost unpicked row of beepers, picking each beeper as it moves.

Question: How can Karel pick the entire field?

Answer: Karel could turn around and move back to the western side of the field, move north one block, face east, and repeat the same actions listed above. Karel could do this for each row of beepers in the field. Since Karel is not standing on a beeper, we will move it to the first beeper before starting to harvest the first row.

If it seems that this idea might work, our next step is to write out the **BEGINNING-OF-EXECUTION/END-OF-EXECUTION** block of the program using English-like new instruction names. We briefly move from planning to *implementing* our plan. Even though this is done on paper, we should still concentrate on correct syntax and proper indenting to reduce errors when we copy our program into the computer.

```
BEGINNING-OF-EXECUTION
  move;
  harvest-1-row;
  return-to-start;
  move-north-1-block;
  harvest-1-row;
  return-to-start;
  move-north-1-block;
  harvest-1-row;
  return-to-start;
  move-north-1-block;
  harvest-1-row;
  return-to-start;
  move-north-1-block;
  harvest-1-row;
  return-to-start;
  move-north-1-block;
  harvest-1-row;
  return-to-start;
  turnoff
END-OF-EXECUTION
```

Before we continue with this plan and begin to work on the new instructions `harvest-1-row`, `return-to-start`, and `move-north-1-block`, we should *analyze* our original plan, looking at its strengths and weaknesses. Our analysis might proceed as follows.

Question: What are the strengths of this plan?

Answer: The plan takes advantage of the new instruction mechanism, and it allows Karel to harvest the beepers.

Question: What are the weaknesses of the plan?

Answer: Karel makes some "empty" trips.

Question: What are these empty trips?

Answer: Karel returns to the starting point on the row that was just harvested.

Question: Can Karel pick more beepers on the way back?

Answer: Instead of harvesting only one row and then turning around and returning to the start, Karel can harvest one row, move north one street, and come back to the west harvesting a second row. Karel can then move one street north to begin the entire process over for the next two rows. If Karel repeats these steps two more times, the entire field of beepers will be harvested.

Again we analyze this new plan for its strengths and weaknesses.

Question: What advantage does this offer over the first plan?

Answer: Karel makes only six trips across the field instead of twelve. There are no empty trips.

Question: What are the weaknesses of this new plan?

Answer: None that we can see.

When we are planning solutions, we should be very critical and not just accept the first plan as the best. We now have two different plans, and you can probably think of several more. Let's avoid the empty trips and implement the second plan.

```
BEGINNING-OF-EXECUTION
  move;
  harvest-2-rows;
  position-for-next-harvest;
  harvest-2-rows;
  position-for-next-harvest;
  harvest-2-rows;
  move;
  turnoff
END-OF-EXECUTION
```

We must now begin to think about planning the new instructions `harvest-2-rows` and `position-for-next-harvest`.

3.8.1.2 The Second Step—Planning `harvest-2-rows` and `position-for-next-harvest`

Our plan contains two subtasks: one harvests two rows, and the other positions Karel to harvest two more rows. The planning of these two subtasks must be just as thorough as the planning was for the overall task. Let's begin with `harvest-2-rows`.

Question: What does `harvest-2-rows` do?

Answer: `harvest-2-rows` must harvest two rows of beepers. One will be harvested as Karel travels east, and the second will be harvested as Karel returns to the west.

Question: What does Karel have to do?

Answer: Karel must pick beepers and move as it travels east. At the end of the row of beepers, Karel must move north one block, face west, and return to the western edge of the field, picking beepers as it travels west.

Continuing to use English-like instruction names, we can now implement this part of the plan.

```
DEFINE-NEW-INSTRUCTION harvest-2-rows AS
  BEGIN
    harvest-1-row-moving-east;
    go-north-to-next-row;
    harvest-1-row-moving-west
  END;
```

We analyze this plan as before, looking for strengths and weaknesses.

Question: What are the strengths of this plan?

Answer: It seems to solve the problem.

Question: What are the weaknesses of this plan?

Answer: Possibly one—we have two different instructions that harvest a single row of beepers.

Question: Do we really need two different harvesting instructions?

Answer: We need one for going east and one for going west.

Question: Do we really need a separate instruction for each direction?

Answer: Harvesting is just a series of **pickbeepers** and **moves**. The direction in which Karel is moving does not matter. If we plan `go-to-next-row` carefully, we can use one instruction to harvest a row of beepers when Karel is going east and the same instruction for going west.

Our analysis shows us that we can reuse a single dictionary entry (`harvest-1-row`) instead of defining two similar instructions, making our program smaller. Here is the new implementation.

```
DEFINE-NEW-INSTRUCTION harvest-2-rows AS
  BEGIN
    harvest-1-row;
    go-to-next-row;
    harvest-1-row
  END;
```

Let's now plan `position-for-next-harvest`.

Question: What does the instruction `position-for-next-harvest` do?

Answer: This instruction is used when Karel is on the western side of the beeper field. It moves the robot north one block and faces Karel east in position to harvest two more rows of beepers.

Question: What does Karel have to do?

Answer: Karel must turn right to face north, move one block, and turn right to face east.

We implement this instruction as follows.

```
DEFINE-NEW-INSTRUCTION position-for-next-harvest AS
  BEGIN
    turnright;
    move;
    turnright
  END;
```

We should analyze this instruction to see if it works properly. Since it seems to work correctly, we are ready to continue our planning and in the process define more new instructions.

3.8.1.3   The Third Step—Planning `harvest-1-row` and
`go-to-next-row`
We now focus our efforts on `harvest-1-row` and finally `go-to-next-row`.

Question: What does `harvest-1-row` do?

Answer: Starting on the first beeper and facing the correct direction, Karel must pick all five beepers, stopping on the location of the last beeper in the row.

Question: What does Karel have to do?

Answer: Karel must execute a sequence of **pickbeeper** and **move** instructions to pick all five beepers in the row.

We can implement **harvest-1-row** as follows.

```
DEFINE-NEW-INSTRUCTION harvest-1-row AS
  BEGIN
    pickbeeper;
    move;
    pickbeeper;
    move;
    pickbeeper;
    move;
    pickbeeper;
    move;
    pickbeeper
  END;
```

We again simulate the instruction, and it seems to work. We now address the instruction **go-to-next-row**.

Question: What does **go-to-next-row** do?

Answer: This instruction moves Karel northward one block to the next row.

Question: Didn't we do that already? Why can't we use **position-for-next-harvest**?[3]

Answer: It will not work properly. When we use **position-for-next-harvest**, Karel must be facing west. Karel is now facing east so **position-for-next-harvest** will not work.

Question: What does Karel have to do?

Answer: Karel must turn left to face north, move one block, and turn left to face west.

The following is the implementation of this new instruction.

```
DEFINE-NEW-INSTRUCTION go-to-next-row AS
  BEGIN
    turnleft;
    move;
    turnleft
  END;
```

---

[3] At this point you should simulate the instruction **position-for-next-harvest** on paper. Start with Karel facing west and see where the robot is when you finish simulating the instruction.

We can use simulation to analyze this instruction and show that it is correct. The only instruction we have left to define is the new instruction `turnright`, which we define as

```
DEFINE-NEW-INSTRUCTION turnright AS
  BEGIN
    turnleft;
    turnleft;
    turnleft
  END;
```

and our program is done.

3.8.1.4   The Final Step—Verifying That the Complete Program Is Correct

Since we have spread this program out over several pages, we print it here so you will find it easier to read and study. Notice that the definition of a new instruction must come before Karel tries to execute that new instruction. This is one of the vagaries of the robot brain. If we mistakenly define an instruction after it is used, Karel will not find the definition.

```
BEGINNING-OF-PROGRAM
  DEFINE-NEW-INSTRUCTION turnright AS
  BEGIN
    turnleft;
    turnleft;
    turnleft
  END;

  DEFINE-NEW-INSTRUCTION go-to-next-row AS
  BEGIN
    turnleft;
    move;
    turnleft
  END;

  DEFINE-NEW-INSTRUCTION harvest-1-row AS
  BEGIN
    pickbeeper;
    move;
    pickbeeper;
    move;
    pickbeeper;
    move;
    pickbeeper;
    move;
    pickbeeper
  END;
```

```
DEFINE-NEW-INSTRUCTION position-for-next-harvest AS
BEGIN
   turnright;
   move;
   turnright
END;

DEFINE-NEW-INSTRUCTION harvest-2-rows AS
BEGIN
   harvest-1-row;
   go-to-next-row;
   harvest-1-row
END;

BEGINNING-OF-EXECUTION
   move;
   harvest-2-rows;
   position-for-next-harvest;
   harvest-2-rows;
   position-for-next-harvest;
   harvest-2-rows;
   move;
   turnoff
END-OF-EXECUTION
END-OF-PROGRAM
```

We are not done. We have used simulation to analyze the individual instructions in the program to see if they work correctly. However, we have not examined how they work in concert as one large robot program. We must now simulate Karel's execution of the entire program to demonstrate that all the parts work correctly to be sure the program is correct. We may have relied on some invalid assumptions when writing the instructions that move Karel between rows, or we may discover some other error in our planning or implementing; maybe our analysis was wrong. A skeptical attitude toward the correctness of our programs will put us in the correct frame of mind for trying to verify them.

Stepwise refinement blends the problem solving activities of planning, implementing, and analyzing into the programming process. It is a powerful programming technique and can shorten the time required to write correct robot programs.

3.8.2   The Design Tree—A Planning Technique

In this section we demonstrate a planning technique called the design tree. Unlike stepwise refinement, which combines the activities of planning, implementing, and analyzing, the design tree involves only planning and analysis; there is no implementation. The design tree is a diagram of our plan. We must warn you that it is a very unusual looking tree, for it grows upside-down with its root at the top and its leaves at the bottom.

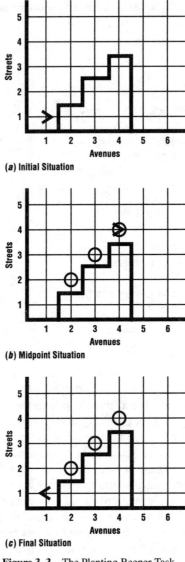

Figure 3–3   The Planting Beeper Task

Figure 3–3 presents an initial, a midpoint, and a final situation. We want Karel to follow the wall "planting" one beeper on the northern side of each east–west wall segment and then return to its original location. In the initial situation, Karel has at least three beepers in the beeper-bag.

3.8.2.1   The First Step—An Overall Plan
We want to plan a solution to this problem using Karel's new instructions in a systematic way. In planning a solution that successfully solves the problem, we must remember that

- Our program must be easy to read and understand;
- Our program must be easy to debug; and
- Our program must be easy to modify in order to solve variations of the original task.

In Section 3.8.1 we learned that it is important first to think about the problem, and then to discuss possible solutions and plan our final solution in English-like terms. Keeping this in mind, we begin our design tree with the root; the root of the tree is simply the **Problem**.

We first examine the overall problem and attempt to divide it into major subtasks, in a process called <u>decomposition</u>. Here is one possible decomposition.

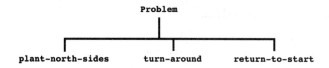

The design tree shows three new instructions: **plant-north-sides**, **turn-around**, and **return-to-start**. These instructions make up the **BEGINNING-OF-EXECUTION/END-OF-EXECUTION** block in our program.

The instruction **plant-north-sides** will move along the wall planting all of the beepers, **turn-around** will turn Karel around for the return trip, and **return-to-start** will move it back to the original location. This tree should be discussed and analyzed for strengths and weaknesses in a manner similar to that used in Section 3.8.1. We must be aware that this is not the only possible decomposition of the problem. There may be others that are just as good or even better. Nonetheless, this is the one we will use for now.

3.8.2.2 The Second Step—Adding More Branches

We now begin work on the second row or *second generation* of the tree, starting on the left side by planning **plant-north-sides**. Can we break **plant-north-sides** into smaller tasks? Look carefully at Karel's movement from its starting position to the place where the first beeper is dropped and envision what must be done to move the robot there. Can we use those same movements to get the robot from the first beeper's spot to the location of the second beeper? Similarly, can we use the same movements to get the robot from that location to the location of the third beeper? The answers to both questions are "yes." We can use one new instruction three times to plant all three beepers. Our design tree will look like this:

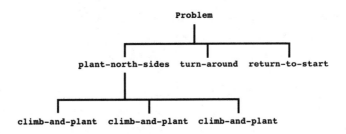

This new branch of the tree corresponds to the **BEGIN/END** block that will comprise the definition of the new instruction **plant-north-sides**.

The **turn-around** instruction must turn Karel 180° and is done using two **turnleft** instructions. Since it requires only primitive instructions, we will add nothing to the tree at this point. We stop drawing new branches in the design tree when we reach the point where we start using only Karel's primitive instructions, as the branches correspond to new instruction definitions.

We can apply the same logic that we used for **plant-north-sides** to the instruction **return-to-start** and break it down in a similar way. Our tree now takes on the following shape.

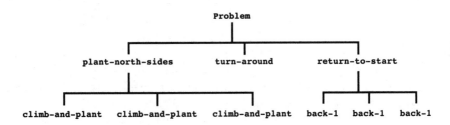

At this point, we believe we have identified all the major subtasks in the original problem. All that should remain is to use the primitive instructions **move**, **turnleft**, and **putbeeper** as needed. We may also have to use the defined instruction, **turnright**, but we consider **turnright** a near-primitive instruction as opposed to a subtask of the problem. Thus, it does not appear in our design tree.

Examine the finished design tree and notice that it has three *levels* or *generations*. The root of the tree is the **Problem**. It has three *children*: **plant-north-sides**, **turn-around**, and **return-to-start**. These three children are *siblings* to each other. Two of these children also have children (**plant-north-sides** and **return-to-start**); one does not (**turn-around**). Continuing the analogy, we find that the instruction **plant-north-sides** is the *parent* of **climb-and-plant**. Similarly, **return-to-start** is the parent of **back-1**. You should also notice that we are using the instruction **climb-and-plant** three times, which is fine. New instructions can be used more than once. In fact, one goal of the design tree process is to identify as many "reusable" new instructions as possible.

3.8.3 Implementing the Plan Using Vertical Slicing

We are now ready to implement the plan (write the program) that we just developed. If we followed what seems natural, we would probably write all the definitions of the new instructions first (e.g., `climb-and-plant`, ...), and then write the instruction names in the `BEGINNING-OF-EXECUTION/END-OF-EXECUTION` block. This is the opposite of the pattern followed by stepwise refinement that was discussed in Section 3.8.1.

To implement the plan, we are going to use a companion technique of the design tree that we call vertical slicing. The overall shape of the design tree is a triangle (Figure 3–4). The top area of the triangle corresponds to the `BEGINNING-OF-EXECUTION/END-OF-EXECUTION` block, and the new instructions that are used are in the lower sections of the triangle.

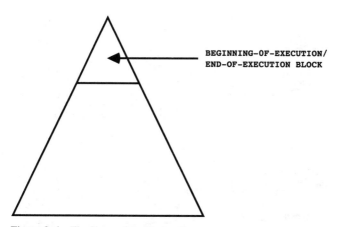

BEGINNING-OF-EXECUTION/
END-OF-EXECUTION BLOCK

Figure 3–4   The Shape of the Design Tree

Vertical slicing sometimes runs against what seems natural. Vertical slicing directs us to implement only the first new instruction used in the `BEGINNING-OF-EXECUTION/END-OF-EXECUTION` block. We then define this new instruction and only those new instructions that are used in this branch of the tree. We are implementing a vertical slice of the tree as shown in Figure 3–5.

We implement only this part of the program because we wish to simplify analysis of the implementation. The technique of stepwise refinement directs us to trace and simulate the instructions to see if they are correct. Vertical slicing tells us to do the same thing, but it allows us to use Karel to help in the process. If we write this small slice of the program, we can have Karel execute it to determine whether there are any execution or intent errors in the slice. We can correct them before we spend time on other slices. This approach lets Karel do some of the testing and reduces the chance of discovering a major flaw in our overall plan just when we think we are done.

Figure 3–5   The Vertical Slice We Implement First

3.8.3.1   The First Slice

To make the first slice, we must return to the design tree. The underlined instructions are the only ones written in our first slice. If a line is drawn from the root of the tree, **Problem**, to the bottom of the tree separating the underlined instructions from the others, we can see the vertical slice that is being implemented.

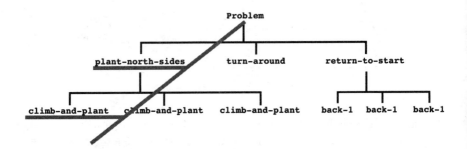

And here is the implementation of the first slice that we test.

```
BEGINNING-OF-PROGRAM
    DEFINE-NEW-INSTRUCTION turnright AS
        BEGIN
            turnleft;
            turnleft;
            turnleft
        END;
```

```
DEFINE-NEW-INSTRUCTION climb-and-plant AS
   BEGIN
      turnleft;
      move;
      turnright;
      move;
      putbeeper
   END;

DEFINE-NEW-INSTRUCTION plant-north-sides AS
   BEGIN
      climb-and-plant
   END;

BEGINNING-OF-EXECUTION
   plant-north-sides;
   turnoff
END-OF-EXECUTION
END-OF-PROGRAM
```

We now carefully analyze the program: we box it to find our syntactic errors, check it for lexical errors, trace it for correct execution, and verify it by simulation. Only then do we have Karel execute it. This program will take Karel up to the corner where the first beeper is placed, put the beeper down, and stop. This is all we need to do to see if the first part of our plan and the implementation of the plan is correct. If Karel turns in the wrong direction, moves too far, or tries to walk into a wall (thus executing an error shutoff), we can correct it before implementing any other instructions.

3.8.3.2   The Second Slice

Once the first slice of the program is correct, we add another slice and test again. This slice should take Karel all the way to the top of the steps, putting one beeper on each of the three steps. The underlined instructions in the tree and the program show this next slice.

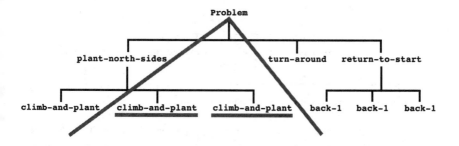

```
BEGINNING-OF-PROGRAM
  DEFINE-NEW-INSTRUCTION turnright AS
    BEGIN
      turnleft;
      turnleft;
      turnleft
    END;

  DEFINE-NEW-INSTRUCTION climb-and-plant AS
    BEGIN
      turnleft;
      move;
      turnright;
      move;
      putbeeper
    END;

  DEFINE-NEW-INSTRUCTION plant-north-sides AS
    BEGIN
      climb-and-plant;
      climb-and-plant;
      climb-and-plant
    END;

  BEGINNING-OF-EXECUTION
    plant-north-sides;
    turnoff
  END-OF-EXECUTION
END-OF-PROGRAM
```

We analyze this program very carefully for errors by boxing, tracing, and simulation. Once we are satisfied it is correct, we again let Karel execute the program.
If the **turnoff** is executed when Karel is in the proper position, we have demonstrated to ourselves that our program is correct to this point. If errors are present,
we find them and correct them.

3.8.3.3 The Third and Fourth Slices
Our next slice is shown in the following tree.

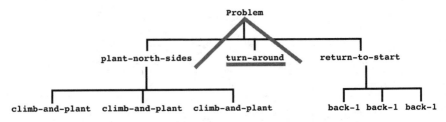

Remember that we want to write our program in small steps. The third slice
will add only the instruction **turn-around**. After implementing this instruction

and analyzing its behavior, Karel should be in the correct position to return to the start.

We can now begin to work on the return trip, and our fourth slice will look like this:

```
BEGINNING-OF-PROGRAM
    DEFINE-NEW-INSTRUCTION turnright AS
        BEGIN
            turnleft;
            turnleft;
            turnleft
        END;

    DEFINE-NEW-INSTRUCTION turn-around AS
        BEGIN
            turnleft;
            turnleft
        END;

    DEFINE-NEW-INSTRUCTION back-1 AS
        BEGIN
            move;
            turnleft;
            move;
            turnright
        END;

    DEFINE-NEW-INSTRUCTION return-to-start AS
        BEGIN
            back-1
        END;

    DEFINE-NEW-INSTRUCTION climb-and-plant AS
        BEGIN
            turnleft;
            move;
            turnright;
            move;
            putbeeper
        END;
```

```
DEFINE-NEW-INSTRUCTION plant-north-sides AS
BEGIN
    climb-and-plant;
    climb-and-plant;
    climb-and-plant
END;

BEGINNING-OF-EXECUTION
    plant-north-sides;
    turn-around;
    return-to-start;
    turnoff
END-OF-EXECUTION
END-OF-PROGRAM
```

We test this program as we have in the earlier implementations and see if Karel stops in the correct place. If it does, we can finish the program and make the final test run.

3.8.3.4   The Last Slice
Here is our final program with the last changes underlined.

```
BEGINNING-OF-PROGRAM
    DEFINE-NEW-INSTRUCTION turnright AS
    BEGIN
        turnleft;
        turnleft;
        turnleft
    END;

    DEFINE-NEW-INSTRUCTION turn-around AS
    BEGIN
        turnleft;
        turnleft
    END;

    DEFINE-NEW-INSTRUCTION back-1 AS
    BEGIN
        move;
        turnleft;
        move;
        turnright
    END;
```

```
DEFINE-NEW-INSTRUCTION return-to-start AS
  BEGIN
    back-1;
    back-1;
    back-1
  END;


DEFINE-NEW-INSTRUCTION climb-and-plant AS
  BEGIN
    turnleft;
    move;
    turnright;
    move;
    putbeeper
  END;


DEFINE-NEW-INSTRUCTION plant-north-sides AS
  BEGIN
    climb-and-plant;
    climb-and-plant;
    climb-and-plant
  END;


BEGINNING-OF-EXECUTION
  plant-north-sides;
  turn-around;
  return-to-start;
  turnoff
END-OF-EXECUTION
END-OF-PROGRAM
```

Writing a program in vertical slices takes away some of the difficulty of testing. If we use the design tree for planning and vertical slicing for implementing, Karel can help us with the testing and relieve us of some of the work.

3.9   ADVANTAGES OF USING NEW INSTRUCTIONS

It is useful to divide a program into small instructions, even if these instructions are executed only once. New instructions nicely structure programs, and English words and phrases make programs more understandable; they help convey the intent of the program. Read back through the programs we have just written and see if you can find any place where they are confusing or difficult to understand.

3.9.1 Avoiding Errors

Many novices think that all of this planning, analyzing, tracing, boxing, and simulating of programs as shown in the previous sections takes too much time. What really takes time is correcting mistakes. These mistakes fall into two broad categories:

- Planning mistakes (execution and intent errors) occur when we write a program without a well-thought-out plan and can waste a lot of programming time. They are usually difficult to fix because large segments of the program may have to be modified or discarded. Careful planning and thorough analysis of the plan can help us avoid planning mistakes.

- Programming mistakes (lexical and syntactic errors) occur when we actually write the program. They can be spelling, punctuation, or other similar errors. If we write the entire program without testing it, we will undoubtedly have many errors to correct, some of which may be multiple instances of the same mistake. Writing the program in slices will both reduce the overall number of errors introduced at any one time and prevent multiple occurrences of the same mistake (e.g., we discover a misspelling of a new instruction name).

Stepwise refinement, the design tree, and vertical slicing are tools that allow us to plan, analyze, and implement our plans in a way that should lead to a robot program containing a minimum of errors.

3.9.2 Future Modifications

Earlier in this chapter we stated that we must write programs that are easy to read and understand, easy to debug, and easy to modify. Karel's world can be readily changed, and we must be able to modify existing programs to keep the robot out of trouble. It is much simpler and takes less time to modify an existing program to perform a slightly different task than to write a completely new one. Below are two situations that differ somewhat from the original one (Figure 3–6).

How difficult would it be to modify our program to accomplish the same beeper-placing task in the new situations? If we are using the design tree for planning, the first problem is easy to solve; we just add a fourth branch to the new instruction **plant-north-sides** as well as a fourth branch to **return-to-start** like this:

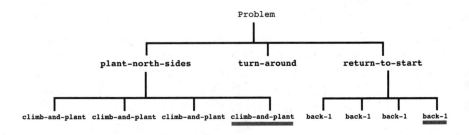

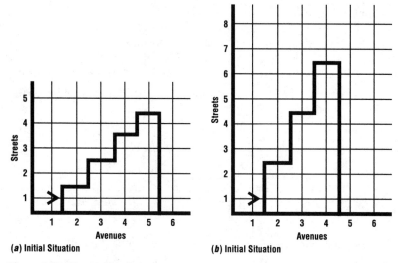

(**a**) Initial Situation   (**b**) Initial Situation

Figure 3–6   Two Modified Worlds

This tree shows us which instructions we should change to solve the new problem. When we change these instructions, we have to add just two new lines to the original program to solve the new task!

What about the second problem? The change here is very different from the change in the first one—we have to modify the instructions that move Karel. The use of new instructions quickly allows us to find where we need to make the change. The only instructions that actually move the robot are `climb-and-plant` and `back-1`. If we make one change in `climb-and-plant` as follows,

```
DEFINE-NEW-INSTRUCTION climb-and-plant AS
  BEGIN
    turnleft;
    move;
    move;  → adding this move is the change
    turnright;
    move;
    putbeeper
  END;
```

we will get Karel to the northernmost wall. If we make a similar change in `back-1`,

```
DEFINE-NEW-INSTRUCTION back-1 AS
  BEGIN
    move;
    turnleft;
    move;
    move;  → adding this move is the change
    turnright
  END;
```

we will get Karel back to the original location.

The use of new instructions also simplifies finding and fixing intent errors. Suppose Karel makes a wrong turn and puts a beeper in the wrong place. Where is the error? If we use new instructions to write our program, and each new instruction performs one specific task (e.g., `climb-and-plant`) or controls a set of related tasks (e.g., `plant-north-sides`), then we can quickly determine the probable location of the error.

3.9.3   A Program Without New Instructions

Below is a program that attempts to solve the original beeper-planting problem with only primitive instructions. Examine the program and ask the same questions we have just explored.

- Where would we change the program to solve the first modified situation?
- Where would we change the program to solve the second modified situation?
- Suppose Karel makes a wrong turn while planting the beepers. Where would we first look to correct the error? As an example, find the single error that we included in this program.

```
BEGINNING-OF-PROGRAM
    BEGINNING-OF-EXECUTION
        turnleft;
        move;
        turnleft;
        turnleft;
        turnleft;
        move;
        putbeeper;
        turnleft;
        move;
        turnleft;
        turnleft;
        turnleft;
        move;
        putbeeper;
        turnleft;
        move;
        turnleft;
        turnleft;
        turnleft;
        move;
        putbeeper;
        turnleft;
```

```
                    turnleft;
                    turnleft;
                    move;
                    turnleft;
                    move;
                    turnleft;
                    turnleft;
                    turnleft;
                    move;
                    turnleft;
                    move;
                    turnleft;
                    turnleft;
                    turnleft;
                    move;
                    turnleft;
                    move;
                    turnleft;
                    turnleft;
                    turnleft;
                    turnoff
              END-OF-EXECUTION
              END-OF-PROGRAM
```

Long lists of instructions such as this one may correctly solve a problem, but they are very difficult to read and understand. They are also very difficult to debug and modify.

3.10 WRITING UNDERSTANDABLE PROGRAMS

Writing understandable programs is as important as writing correct ones. Some say that it is even more important. This group argues that most programs initially have a few errors and that understandable programs are easier to debug. Good programmers are distinguished from bad ones by their ability to write clear and concise programs that someone else can read and quickly understand. What makes a program easy to understand? We offer two criteria:

- A good program is the simple composition of easily understandable parts. Each part of the programs we just wrote can be understood by itself. Even without a detailed understanding of the parts, the plans that the programs use to accomplish their respective tasks are also easy to understand.

- Dividing a program (or a large instruction definition) into small, easy to understand pieces is not enough. We must also make sure to name our new instructions properly. These names provide a description, possibly the only description, of what the instruction does. Imagine what the previous programs would look like, if for each meaningful instruction name we had used a name like `first-instruction` or `do-it-now`. Karel allows us to choose any instruction names we desire, but with this freedom comes the responsibility to select accurate and descriptive names.

It is much easier to verify or debug a program that contains new instructions. The following two facts support this claim.

- New instructions can be independently tested. When writing a program, we should test each instruction immediately after it is written, until we are convinced that it is correct. Then we can forget how the instruction works and just remember what the instruction does. Remembering should be easy, if we name the instruction accurately.

- New instructions impose a structure on our programs, and we can use this structure to help us locate bugs. When debugging a program, we should first find which of the new instructions is malfunctioning. Then we can concentrate on debugging that instruction, ignoring the other parts of our program, which are irrelevant to the bug.

Thus, we see that there is an interesting psychological phenomenon related to Karel's instruction definition mechanism. Because the human brain can focus on only a limited amount of information at any one time, the ability to ignore details that are no longer relevant is a great aid to program writing and debugging.

To help make our new instruction definitions understandable, we should also keep their lengths within a reasonable range. A good rule of thumb is that definitions should rarely exceed five to ten instructions. This limit leaves us enough room to write a meaningful instruction, but it restrains us from cramming too much detail into any one definition. If an instruction's size exceeds this limit, we should divide it into a set of smaller instructions. This rule applies to the number of instructions written within the **BEGINNING-OF-EXECUTION/END-OF-EXECUTION** block too. Most novice programmers tend to write instruction definitions that are too large. It is better to write many small, well-named instructions instead of a few oversized definitions.

Writing understandable programs with new instructions and using the techniques of stepwise refinement, the design tree, and vertical slicing can reduce the number of errors we make and the amount of time we spend writing robot programs.

3.11 PROBLEM SET

The problems in this section require defining new instructions for Karel or writing complete programs that include dictionary entries. Concentrate on writing well-structured programs, and build from naturally descriptive new instructions. Practice using stepwise refinement and freely define any new instructions that you need. If you find yourself continually writing the same sequence of instructions, it is a sure sign that you need to define that sequence as a new instruction. Carefully check for syntactic errors in your program, and simulate Karel's execution of each program to verify that it is correct.

Paradoxically, the programs in this problem set will be among the largest you write. The instructions covered in the next chapters are so powerful that we will find that complex tasks can be solved with programs comprising a small number of these potent instructions.

1. Write appropriate definitions for the following new instructions: (1) `turn-around`, which turns Karel around 180°; (2) `move-mile`, remembering that miles are eight blocks long; (3) `move-backward`, which moves Karel one block backward but leaves it facing the same direction; and (4) `move-kilo-mile`, which moves Karel 1000 miles forward. This last problem is difficult, but a fairly short solution does exist. You may use the `move-mile` instruction in this problem without redefining it. In addition, which of these four instructions might cause an error shutoff when it is executed?

2. Karel sometimes works as a pin-setter in a bowling alley. Write a program that instructs Karel to transform the initial situation in Figure 3–7 into the final situation. Karel starts this task with ten beepers in the beeper-bag.

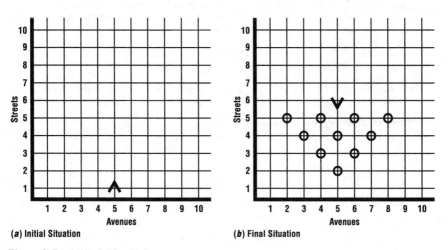

(*a*) Initial Situation   (*b*) Final Situation

Figure 3–7   A Pin-Setting Task

3. Copy the complete program written in the stepwise refinement section and box it. Make sure that your boxes do not overlap and that semicolons appear only between adjacent boxes.

4. Rewrite the harvesting program using a different stepwise refinement.

5. Figure 3–8 illustrates a field of beepers that Karel planted one night after a baseball game. Write a program that harvests all these beepers. *Hint*: This task is not too different from the harvesting example. If you see the correspondence between these two harvesting tasks, you should be able to develop a program for this task that is similar to the original harvesting program.

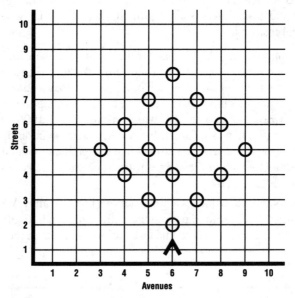

Figure 3–8   Another Harvesting Task

6. Karel wants to send greetings to the other inhabitants of the universe, so the robot needs to plant a field of beepers that broadcasts the message to alien astronomers. Program Karel to plant the message of beepers shown in Figure 3–9. You may choose Karel's starting position.

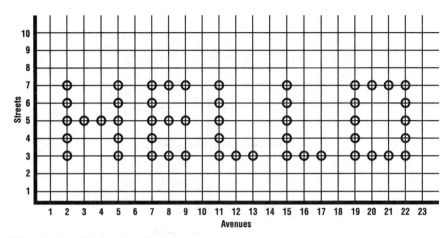

Figure 3–9   A Message for Alien Astronomers

7. Karel has received a contract from NASA (the National Aeronautics and Space Administration) to display the correct time for astronauts to read as they orbit above Karel's world. The time must be displayed digitally and must fit in the situation shown in Figure 3–10. You may choose the size and shape of the digits. The program must allow you to quickly change the time so that Karel can rapidly update the display. For practice, display the time 1052.

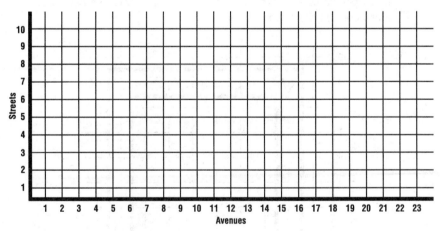

Figure 3–10   A Digital Clock

8. Karel has taken a part-time job as a gardener. Karel's specialty is planting beepers. Karel's current task is to plant one and only one beeper on each corner around the "+" shaped wall arrangement in the situation shown in Figure 3–11.

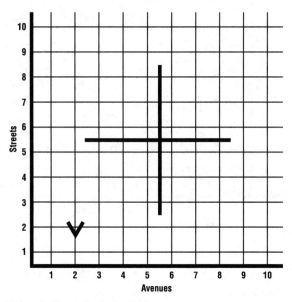

Figure 3–11   A Gardening Task

9.   Karel's beeper crop in Problem 3.11–8 failed, so the robot decided to try a different part-time job. The robot now installs carpets (made from beepers) in buildings in its world. Write a program that instructs Karel to install a carpet in the building shown in Figure 3–12. There must be no "lumps" in the carpet, so be sure that Karel places one and only one beeper on each intersection in the room.

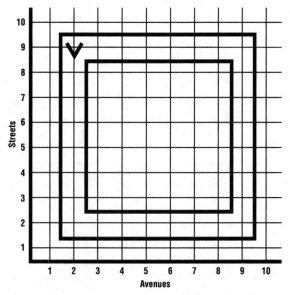

Figure 3–12   A Carpeting Task

10.   Program Karel to arrange beepers as shown in the final situation given in Figure 3–13. Karel has exactly 12 beepers in its beeper-bag.

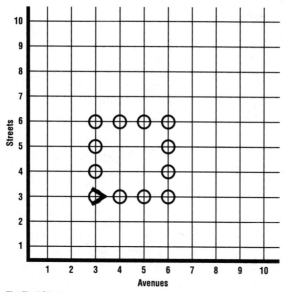

The Final Situation

Figure 3–13   A Box of Beepers

4 CONDITIONALLY EXECUTING INSTRUCTIONS

In the preceding chapters, Karel's exact initial situation was known at the start of a task. When we wrote our programs, this information allowed Karel to find beepers and avoid running into walls. However, these programs worked only in their specific initial situations. If Karel tried to execute one of these programs in a slightly different initial situation, the robot would almost certainly perform an error shutoff.

What Karel needs is the ability to survey its local environment and then, on the basis of that information, decide what to do next. The **IF** instructions discussed in this chapter—there are two versions, the **IF/THEN** and the **IF/THEN/ELSE**—provide Karel with this decision ability. Both allow Karel to test its environment and, depending on the result of the test, decide which instruction to execute next. The **IF** instructions enable us to write much more general programs for Karel, which accomplish the same task in a variety of similar, but different, initial situations.

4.1 THE `IF/THEN` INSTRUCTION

The **IF/THEN** instruction is the simpler of the two **IF** variants. It has the following general form.

```
IF  <test>  THEN
    <instruction>
```

The **IF/THEN** instruction introduces the two new reserved words **IF** and **THEN**. The reserved word **IF** signals Karel that an **IF** instruction is present, and the reserved word **THEN** separates <test> from <instruction>. The <instruction> is known as the **THEN** clause of the instruction. We indent the **IF/THEN** instruction as shown, to highlight the fact that <instruction> is a component of the **IF** instruction.

Karel executes the **IF/THEN** instruction by first checking whether <**test**> is true or false in its current situation. If <**test**> is true, Karel executes <**instruction**>; if <**test**> is false, Karel ignores <**instruction**>. In either case, Karel is then finished executing the entire **IF/THEN** instruction. For an example, let's look at the program fragment[1] below, which consists of an **IF/THEN** instruction followed by a **move** instruction. (Notice the placement of the semicolon between the entire **IF** instruction and the following **move** instruction.)

```
IF next-to-a-beeper   THEN
     pickbeeper;
move
```

Karel executes this **IF/THEN** instruction by first checking whether it is next to (on the same corner as) a beeper. If Karel finds that **next-to-a-beeper** is true, the robot executes the **THEN** clause, which instructs it to execute **pickbeeper**. Karel is now finished executing the **IF/THEN** instruction and continues by executing the rest of the program starting at the **move** instruction.

Now suppose that there are no beepers on the corner when Karel executes this program fragment. In this case **next-to-a-beeper** is false, so Karel does not execute the **THEN** clause. Instead, it skips directly to the **move** instruction and continues executing the program from there. The result of this second case is that Karel executes the **IF/THEN** instruction by doing nothing more than checking whether or not it is next to a beeper. An error shutoff cannot occur in either case, because Karel executes the **pickbeeper** instruction only if it confirms the presence of at least one beeper on the corner.

4.2 THE CONDITIONS KAREL CAN TEST

In Chapter 1 we briefly discussed Karel's sensory capabilities. We learned that the robot can see walls, hear beepers, determine which direction it is facing, and feel if there are any beepers in its beeper-bag. The conditions that Karel can test are divided according to these same four categories. What follows is a complete list of the conditions that can be substituted for the bracketed word <**test**> in an **IF/THEN** instruction.

For purposes of classification, Karel treats these words much like primitive instructions; hence, they are written using lower-case letters. Also notice that each condition is available in both its positive and negative form (for example, **front-is-clear** and **front-is-blocked**).

- **front-is-clear,**   **front-is-blocked,**
  left-is-clear,   **left-is-blocked,**
  right-is-clear,   **right-is-blocked.**

---

[1]To conserve space, we often demonstrate a programming idea without writing a complete robot program or new instruction. Instead, we just write the necessary instructions, which are called a program fragment.

- next-to-a-beeper,   not-next-to-a-beeper.
- facing-north,   not-facing-north,
  facing-south,   not-facing-south,
  facing-east,   not-facing-east,
  facing-west,   not-facing-west.
- any-beepers-in-beeper-bag, no-beepers-in-beeper-bag.

Remember that Karel has three television cameras for eyes, each focused to detect walls exactly half a block away. One camera is facing directly ahead, one is facing to the left, and one is facing to the right. Karel tests **right-is-clear**, for example, by checking its right television camera for the presence of a wall.

The **next-to-a-beeper** test is true when Karel is on the same corner as one or more beepers. Karel cannot hear beepers any farther away, and it obviously cannot hear beepers that are in the soundproof beeper-bag.

Karel consults its internal compass to determine what direction it is facing. Finally, Karel can test whether or not there are any beepers in the beeper-bag by probing it with the mechanical arm.

4.3 SIMPLE EXAMPLES OF THE IF/THEN INSTRUCTION

This section examines three new instructions that use the **IF/THEN** instruction. During our discussion of the second definition, we explain what happens when a necessary **BEGIN/END** block is omitted from a **THEN** clause. We will also discuss how **IF/THEN** instructions are boxed.

4.3.1 The harvest-1-row Instruction

Recall the harvesting task that was discussed in Section 3.8.1. Karel's new task still requires the robot to harvest the same-size field, but this time there is no guarantee that a beeper is on each corner of the field. Because Karel's original program for this task would cause an error shutoff when it tried to execute a **pickbeeper** on any barren corner, we must modify it to avoid executing illegal **pickbeeper** instructions. Karel must harvest a beeper only if it determines that one is present.

Knowing about Karel's **IF/THEN** instruction, we can now write a program for this slightly more general task. One sample initial situation is illustrated in Figure 4–1.

Please notice that this is only one of many possible initial situations. Our program must be able to harvest this size field (six by five) regardless of which corners have beepers and which do not. Luckily for us, almost all of our previously written harvesting program can be reused—another advantage of clear and clean programming. All we need to do is modify the **harvest-1-row** instruction by replacing **pickbeeper** with **pickbeeper-if-present**.

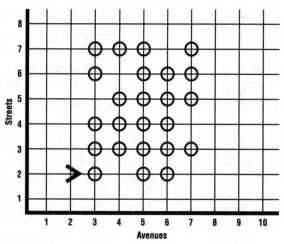

Initial Situation

Figure 4–1 A Modified Harvest Task—not all corners have beepers

```
DEFINE-NEW-INSTRUCTION harvest-1-row AS
BEGIN
  pickbeeper-if-present;
  move;
  pickbeeper-if-present;
  move;
  pickbeeper-if-present;
  move;
  pickbeeper-if-present;
  move;
  pickbeeper-if-present
END;
```

Of course, we must also write the **pickbeeper-if-present** instruction, but this is easily done by using the **IF/THEN** instruction.

```
DEFINE-NEW-INSTRUCTION pickbeeper-if-present AS
BEGIN
  IF next-to-a-beeper   THEN
    pickbeeper
END;
```

We should note that the **BEGIN/END** block surrounding the definition of **pickbeeper-if-present** is unnecessary because the definition contains only one instruction—the **IF/THEN**. The **pickbeeper** within the **THEN** clause is part of the encompassing **IF** instruction. We follow the convention of always defining a new instruction by enclosing its definition in a **BEGIN/END** block, and we recommend that you do likewise.

4.3.2 The `face-north-if-facing-south` Instruction

This section demonstrates how we decide when to use the **IF/THEN** instruction and how we decide what condition we want Karel to check in <**test**>. As part of this and future discussions, let's assume we are planning and implementing the solution to a large problem where Karel is on a treasure hunt for the "*Lost Beeper Mine*" which is a very large pile of beepers.

Let's further assume that we have developed an overall plan and are working on one small task within this plan. This task requires that Karel face to the north only if the robot is currently facing south. In Chapter 3 we introduced a question and answer format to show how we might plan and analyze possible ways to solve a problem. The same format also works well in the implementing phase of problem solving.

Question: What does Karel have to do?

Answer: Karel must turn to face north only if it is currently facing south.

Question: How many alternatives does the robot have to choose from?

Answer: Two.

Question: What are these alternatives?

Answer: Alternative #1 is to turn to the north if it is facing south.
Alternative #2 is to do nothing if it is facing any other direction.

Question: What instruction can we use to allow Karel to decide which alternative to choose?

Answer: The **IF/THEN** instruction allows Karel to decide which alternative to choose.

Question: What test can Karel use in the **IF/THEN** instruction?

Answer: Since Karel is supposed to turn to the north only if it is facing to the south, the test **facing-south** can be used.

Question: What does Karel do if it is facing south?

Answer: Karel will turn left two times to face north.

Question: What does Karel do if it is not facing south?

Answer: Karel does nothing.

The thought process for implementing each instruction definition in our program must be as careful and detailed as it was when we were developing our original plan for the solution. Each step must be carefully analyzed for its strengths and weaknesses. If we ask a question and we cannot answer it satisfactorily, then either we have asked the wrong question or our plan for the instruction's definition is flawed. The longer we spend thinking about the implementation, the less time we will spend correcting errors. Having taken the time to analyze our answers, we will have an instruction implementation that looks like this.

```
DEFINE-NEW-INSTRUCTION   face-north-if-facing-south   AS
   BEGIN
      IF   facing-south   THEN
         BEGIN
            turnleft;
            turnleft
         END
   END;
```

Notice that the form of this **IF/THEN** instruction is slightly different from the previous one. The <**instruction**> has been replaced by a **BEGIN/END** block. Remember that Karel interprets a **BEGIN/END** block as a single instruction. We suggest that you use a **BEGIN/END** block as the **THEN** clause regardless of the number of actual instructions to be executed. The **BEGIN/END** block can help us read the program, and Karel does not care if "extra" **BEGIN/END** blocks are in the program. Also remember that indentation is used to help us read the program.

4.3.3   The `face-north` Instruction

Here is a new problem to solve. Let's assume we are planning the definition of another part of the *Lost Beeper Mine* problem. We must implement an instruction definition that faces Karel north regardless of the direction it is currently facing. Using the question/answer format, we approach this solution by first thinking about Karel's situation. Can we use the information about the direction Karel is currently facing to solve the problem?

Question: What does Karel have to do?

Answer: It must determine which direction it is facing to decide how many **turnlefts** to execute so it will be facing north.

Question: How many different alternatives does the robot have?

Answer: Karel has one alternative for each direction it could be facing. Therefore, it has four alternatives.

Question: What are these alternatives?

Answer: Alternative #1 facing north—do nothing.
Alternative #2 facing east—turn left one time.
Alternative #3 facing south—turn left two times.
Alternative #4 facing west—turn left three times.

Question: What test(s) can Karel use to determine which direction it is facing?

Answer: Karel can check to see if it is facing east, facing south, or facing west. Since Karel does not have to do anything when it is facing north, we do not have to use that test.

We can use these questions and their answers to aid us in implementing the new instruction, `face-north`.

```
DEFINE-NEW-INSTRUCTION  face-north  AS
  BEGIN
    IF facing-east  THEN
      turnleft;
    IF facing-south  THEN
      BEGIN
        turnleft;
        turnleft
      END;
    IF facing-west  THEN
      BEGIN
        turnleft;
        turnleft;
        turnleft
      END
  END;
```

Compare this instruction to the set of questions preceding it. Did we ask all of the questions needed? Did we answer them correctly? Trace this instruction for execution and simulate it four times, one for each direction Karel could initially be facing. Does it work in all cases?

There is another way to solve this problem. Examine this set of questions.

Question: What does Karel have to do?

Answer: Karel must turn left until it is facing north.

Question: How many alternatives does the robot have?

Answer: Two.

Question: What are they?

Answer: Alternative #1 is to turn left if it is not facing north. Alternative # 2 is to do nothing if it is already facing north.

Question: How can we use this information?

Answer: Karel can never be more than three **turnlefts** away from facing north, so we can use a sequence of three **IF/THEN** instructions; each one will check to see if Karel is **not-facing-north**. If the test is true, Karel will turn left and be one **turnleft** closer to facing north.

Question: What happens when Karel starts out facing north?

Answer: All three tests will be false, and Karel does nothing.

Question: What happens when Karel is facing east?

Answer: The first test is true, and Karel executes a **turnleft**. The remaining two tests are false, and Karel does nothing.

Question: What happens when Karel is facing south?

Answer: The first two tests are true, so Karel executes two **turnlefts**. The third test is false, and its **THEN** clause is skipped.

Question: What happens when Karel is facing west?

Answer: All three tests will be true, so Karel will execute three **turnlefts**.

Here is our resulting new instruction.

```
DEFINE-NEW-INSTRUCTION  face-north AS
  BEGIN
    IF not-facing-north  THEN
       turnleft;
    IF not-facing-north  THEN
       turnleft;
    IF not-facing-north  THEN
       turnleft
  END;
```

Trace this instruction for execution and simulate it four times, one for each direction Karel could initially be facing. Does it work in all cases?

The question must be asked as to which of these two **face-north** instructions is better. For now, either is perfectly acceptable.

4.3.4 Boxing the IF/THEN Instruction

Boxing an **IF/THEN** instruction is similar to boxing a dictionary entry, because both use reserved words to separate their different components. Karel boxes the **IF/THEN** instruction by first boxing <**test**>, then boxing the instruction inside the **THEN** clause (which may be a single instruction or a **BEGIN/END** block), and finally boxing the entire **IF/THEN** instruction. This last big box includes the reserved words **IF** and **THEN**, the previously boxed test, and the previously boxed **THEN** clause. Study the two slightly different versions of **capture-the-beeper** that follow. (The numbers again indicate Karel's order of boxing.) See if you can find the difference between the examples.

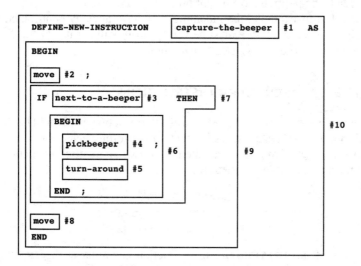

This first definition contains three instructions: the first **move**, the **IF/THEN**, and the second **move**. Each of these instructions is separated from the next by a semicolon, and the two instructions inside the **BEGIN/END** block in the **THEN** clause are also separated by a semicolon.

Here is a slightly different version of the definition.

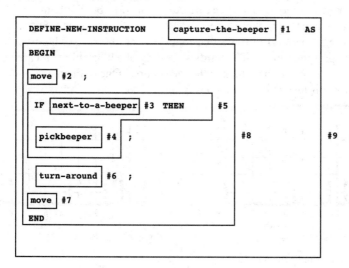

There is a major difference between the two definitions; the second definition does not have a **BEGIN/END** block as its **THEN** clause. Its **THEN** clause consists only of the **pickbeeper** instruction. Karel executes the **turn-around** instruction regardless of the result of the **next-to-a-beeper** test. If you look quickly at the code, the two definitions may seem to be identical, primarily because of the way the instructions are indented. However, our indenting means nothing to Karel when it reads the program. We indent programs solely to make it easier for us to read them. In this example, the indenting may have actually contributed to our misreading the definition. We must be very careful with our use of **BEGIN/END** blocks when we write an **IF/THEN** instruction.

4.4   THE **IF/THEN/ELSE** INSTRUCTION

In this section we discuss the second type of **IF** instruction that is built into Karel's vocabulary. The **IF/THEN/ELSE** instruction is useful when, depending on the result of some test, Karel must execute one of two alternative instructions. The general form of the **IF/THEN/ELSE** is

```
IF <test>   THEN
      <instruction-1>
ELSE <instruction-2>
```

The form of the **IF/THEN/ELSE** instruction is similar to the **IF/THEN** instruction, except that it includes an **ELSE** clause. Karel's punctuation rules require that no semicolon be placed before the reserved word **ELSE**. Karel executes an **IF/THEN/ELSE** in much the same manner as an **IF/THEN**. It first determines whether <test> is true or false in the current situation. If <test> is true, Karel executes <instruction-1>; if <test> is false, Karel executes <instruction-2>. Thus, depending on its current situation, Karel executes either <instruction-1> or <instruction-2>, but not both.

Let's look at a task that uses the **IF/THEN/ELSE** instruction. Suppose that we want to program Karel to run a one-mile-long hurdle race, where vertical wall sections represent hurdles. The hurdles are only one block high and are randomly placed between any two corners in the race course. One of the many possible race courses for this task is illustrated in Figure 4–2.

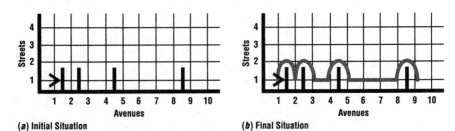

(a) Initial Situation   **(b) Final Situation**

Figure 4–2   A Hurdle Jumping Race

Karel could easily run this race by jumping between every pair of corners, but although this strategy is simple to program, it would slow the robot down too much. Instead, we must program Karel to move straight ahead when it can and to jump over hurdles only when it must. The program implementing this strategy consists of a **BEGINNING-OF-EXECUTION/END-OF-EXECUTION** block that contains eight **race-stride** instructions followed by a **turnoff**. The definition of **race-stride** can be written using stepwise refinement as follows.

```
DEFINE-NEW-INSTRUCTION race-stride AS
BEGIN
    IF front-is-clear  THEN
        move
    ELSE  jump-hurdle
END;
```

We continue our refinement by writing **jump-hurdle**.

```
DEFINE-NEW-INSTRUCTION jump-hurdle AS
BEGIN
    jump-up;
    move;
    jump-down
END;
```

Finally, we write **jump-up** and **jump-down**, the instructions needed to complete the definition of **jump-hurdle**.

```
DEFINE-NEW-INSTRUCTION jump-up AS
BEGIN
    turnleft;
    move;
    turnright
END;
```

and

```
DEFINE-NEW-INSTRUCTION jump-down AS
BEGIN
    turnright;
    move;
    turnleft
END;
```

Of course, the definitions of **jump-up** and **jump-down** must precede **jump-hurdle** in the complete program, and the definition of the ubiquitous **turnright** instruction must also be included. To verify that these instructions are correct, we must finish writing the program and then simulate Karel's running of the race shown in Figure 4-2.

4.5 NESTED `IF` INSTRUCTIONS

Although we have seen a large number of `IF` instructions, we have ignored an entire class of complex `IF`'s. These are known as nested `IF` instructions, because they are written with an `IF` instruction nested inside the `THEN` or `ELSE` clause of another `IF`. No new execution rules are needed to simulate nested `IF`'s, but a close adherence to the established rules is required. Simulating nested `IF` instructions is sometimes difficult because it is easy for us to lose track of where we are in the instruction. The following discussion should be read carefully and understood completely as an example of how to test instructions that include nested `IF`'s.

To demonstrate a nested `IF` instruction, we propose a task that redistributes beepers in a field. This task requires that Karel traverse a field and leave exactly one beeper on each corner. The robot must plant a beeper on each barren corner and remove one beeper from every corner where two beepers are present. All corners in this task are constrained to have zero, one, or two beepers on them. One sample initial and final situation is displayed in Figure 4–3. In these situations, multiple beepers on a corner are represented by a number. We can assume that Karel has enough beepers in its beeper-bag to replant the necessary number of corners.

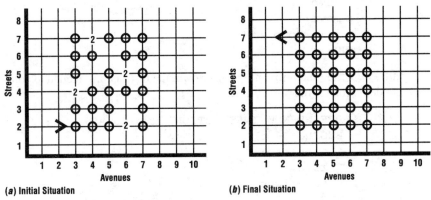

(*a*) Initial Situation   (*b*) Final Situation

Figure 4–3   A Beeper Replanting Task

The heart of the program that solves this task is an instruction that enables Karel to satisfy the one-beeper requirement for each corner. Here is the instruction.

```
DEFINE-NEW-INSTRUCTION replant-exactly-one-beeper AS
   BEGIN
      IF not-next-to-a-beeper   THEN
         putbeeper
      ELSE
         BEGIN
            pickbeeper;
            IF not-next-to-a-beeper THEN
               putbeeper
         END
   END;
```

The following is a boxed version of the same definition for easier reading and simulation.

```
DEFINE-NEW-INSTRUCTION replant-exactly-one-beeper AS
  BEGIN
    IF not-next-to-a-beeper THEN
      putbeeper
    ELSE
      BEGIN
        pickbeeper ;
        IF not-next-to-a-beeper THEN
          putbeeper
      END
  END
```

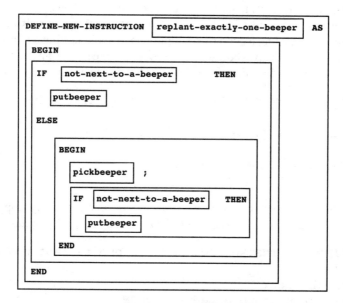

The *outer* **IF** in this definition is an **IF/THEN/ELSE**, and the *nested* **IF** is an **IF/THEN**. The nested **IF** instruction is inside the **ELSE** clause of the outer **IF**. Next, we simulate Karel in the three possible corner situations: an empty corner, a corner with one beeper, and a corner with two beepers.

In the empty corner situation, Karel executes the outer **IF** and determines that the test is true. The robot executes the **putbeeper** instruction in the **THEN** clause, placing one beeper on the corner. Karel has now finished executing the outer **IF** instruction and thus has finished executing **replant-exactly-one-beeper**.

Next, we assume that there is one beeper on Karel's corner. Karel first executes the outer **IF**. Because the test is false, the robot executes the **ELSE** clause. This clause is a **BEGIN/END** block comprised of two instructions, **pickbeeper** and the nested **IF** instruction. Karel picks the beeper and performs the test associated with the nested **IF**. The test is true, so Karel executes the **THEN** clause of this **IF** instruction and puts a beeper back on the empty corner. Karel is now finished with the nested **IF**, the **BEGIN/END** block of the **ELSE** clause, the outer **IF**, and the entire **replant-exactly-one-beeper** instruction.

Finally, we assume that Karel is on a corner with two beepers. Karel executes the outer **IF**, finds the test is false, and then executes the **ELSE** clause. Karel picks up one of the two beepers on the corner. Up to this point, Karel has duplicated its actions in the one-beeper situation, but now comes the difference in execution. Karel executes the nested **IF** instruction, finds the test is false, and skips the nested **IF**'s **THEN** clause. Once again, Karel is now finished with the nested **IF**, the **BEGIN/END** block of the **ELSE** clause, the outer **IF**, and the entire **replant-exactly-one-beeper** instruction.

When nested **IF** instructions seem too intricate, we should try replacing the nested **IF** with a new instruction name. The definition of this auxiliary instruction must command Karel to perform the same actions as the nested **IF** and may help us better understand what Karel is doing. Because nesting also makes an instruction less readable, a good rule of thumb is to avoid nesting **IF** instructions more than one level deep. The **replant-exactly-one-beeper** instruction, which has one level of nesting, is rewritten below using an auxiliary instruction.

```
DEFINE-NEW-INSTRUCTION replant-exactly-one-beeper AS
BEGIN
   IF not-next-to-a-beeper   THEN
      putbeeper
   ELSE   next-to-one-replant-one
END;
```

We write the **next-to-one-replant-one** instruction by copying the **ELSE** clause from our original definition of **replant-exactly-one-beeper**.

```
DEFINE-NEW-INSTRUCTION next-to-one-replant-one AS
BEGIN
   pickbeeper;
   IF not-next-to-a-beeper   THEN
      putbeeper
END;
```

Given the entire program from Section 3.8.1 along with either of these new definitions of the **replant-exactly-one-beeper** instruction, do we have a correct solution for the beeper replanting task? We may consider using our old method of verification and test the program with Karel in every possible initial situation, but there are over 200 trillion[2] different fields that this program must be able to replant correctly! It would be ludicrous to attempt verification by exhaustively testing Karel in every possible initial situation.

Instead, we will settle for probable correctness based on the following informal argument: (1) we have verified that **replant-exactly-one-beeper** works correctly on any corner that is empty or contains one or two beepers, and (2) we can easily verify that our program commands Karel to execute this instruction on each corner of the field. Therefore, we conclude that the program correctly replants the entire field.

This argument further enhances the claim that Karel's mechanism for instruction definition is a powerful aid to programming. In general, we can informally conclude that an entire program is correct by verifying that (1) each new instruction in the program works correctly in all possible situations in which it can be

---

[2]There are three different possibilities for each corner, and there are thirty corners in the field. The total number of different fields is thus 3 multiplied by itself 30 times. For you mathemagicians, the exact number of different fields is 205,891,132,094,649.

executed, and (2) the program executes each new instruction at the appropriate time. This method allows us to verify a program by splitting it into separate, simpler verifications—just as stepwise refinement allows us to write a program by splitting it into separate, simpler instructions.

4.6   MORE COMPLEX TESTS

It is not a trivial matter to have Karel make two or more tests at the same time. More sophisticated programming languages provide the capability to make multiple tests within an **IF/THEN** or an **IF/THEN/ELSE** instruction. We can do this, but we must be clever with our programming as illustrated by the following example.

Let's assume we are still working on the *Lost Beeper Mine* problem introduced earlier. Recall that the *Lost Beeper Mine* is a very large pile of beepers. We have another assignment from that problem—a very important landmark along the way is found where all of the following are true:

- Karel is facing west;
- Karel's right side is blocked;
- Karel's left side is blocked;
- Karel's front is clear; and
- there is at least one beeper on the corner;

Following these requirements, we must plan an instruction that will test all of these conditions simultaneously. If we do what seems logical, we might try to write something like this:

```
IF    facing-west
AND   right-is-blocked
AND   left-is-blocked
AND   front-is-clear
AND   next-to-a-beeper    THEN
          <instruction>
```

This seems very logical, but there is one major problem—Karel does not understand "**AND**." Because the "**AND**" will result in a lexical error, we must use a sequence of nested **IF/THEN** instructions to do the job.

```
IF  facing-west  THEN
  IF  right-is-blocked  THEN
    IF  left-is-blocked   THEN
      IF  front-is-clear    THEN
        IF  next-to-a-beeper  THEN
              <instruction>
```

If we trace this, we will find that all the tests must evaluate to true before Karel can execute < **instruction**>.

4.7 WHEN TO USE AN IF INSTRUCTION

Thus far, we have spent most of our time and effort in this chapter explaining how the IF/THEN and the IF/THEN/ELSE instructions work. It is at this point that students are usually told, *"Write a program that uses the IF/THEN and the IF/THEN/ELSE instruction so that Karel can ..."* It is also at this point that we hear the following question being asked by students, *"I understand how these work, but I don't understand when to use them."* It is "understanding when to use them" that is the focus of this section.

Let's review what the IF/THEN and the IF/THEN/ELSE instructions allow Karel to do in a robot program:

- The IF/THEN instruction allows Karel to decide whether to execute or skip entirely the instruction or block of instructions within the THEN clause.
- The IF/THEN/ELSE instruction allows Karel to decide whether to execute the instruction or block of instructions in the THEN clause or the ELSE clause.
- Nesting these instructions allows Karel to make more complex choices if required.

We can use these three statements to build a decision map. A decision map is a technique that asks questions about the problem we are trying to solve. The answers to the questions determine the branch we follow through the map. Figure 4-4 shows the section of the decision map that a programmer would use for choosing between an IF/THEN and an IF/THEN/ELSE.

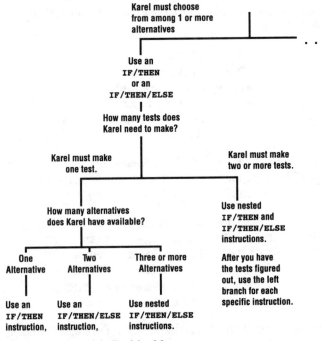

Figure 4–4   Part of the Decision Map

To use this part of the decision map, we must be at a point during our implementation where Karel needs to choose from among one or more alternatives. We use the map by asking each question as we encounter it and following the path that has the answer. If done correctly, we eventually arrive at an implementation suggestion. If the map does not work, we probably do not need to choose between alternatives or we have not correctly thought out our plan.

Suppose Karel must face north if there is a beeper on the current corner and face south otherwise. How many tests does Karel have to make? One—either **next-to-a-beeper** or **not-next-to-a-beeper**. This answer directs us down the left path to the next question, how many alternatives does Karel have available? Two—Karel must either face north or face south. This takes us down the path to the **IF/THEN/ELSE** instruction. Our implementation looks like this.

```
IF next-to-a-beeper  THEN
    face-north
ELSE
    face-south
```

4.8 TRANSFORMATIONS FOR SIMPLIFYING IF INSTRUCTIONS

This section discusses four useful transformations that help us simplify programs containing **IF** instructions. We start by observing that when two program fragments result in Karel's performing exactly the same actions, we call this pair of fragments execution equivalent. For a simple example, **turnleft; putbeeper** is execution equivalent to **putbeeper; turnleft**.

In general, we can create one execution equivalent **IF/THEN/ELSE** instruction from another by replacing <**test**> with its opposite and interchanging the **THEN** and the **ELSE** clauses as illustrated below. We call this transformation test reversal. Notice that if we perform test reversal twice on the same instruction, we get back to the instruction with which we started.

```
IF  front-is-clear THEN        IF front-is-blocked  THEN
    move                           jump-hurdle
ELSE  jump-hurdle              ELSE  move
```

Test reversal can be used to help novice programmers overcome the following difficulty. Suppose that we start to write an **IF** instruction and get ourselves into the dilemma illustrated below on the left. The problem is that we want Karel to do nothing special when its front is clear,[3] but when its front is blocked we want Karel to execute <**instruction**>. We would like to remove the **THEN** clause, but doing so would cause a syntactic error—Karel does not understand an **IF/ELSE** instruction. The solution to our problem is illustrated on the right.

---

[3] We can define the instruction **do-nothing** as four left turns. Executing this instruction would leave Karel's position unchanged, and this instruction is also immune to error shutoffs.

```
IF  front-is-clear THEN     IF front-is-blocked  THEN
    do-nothing                  <instruction>
ELSE  <instruction>
```

To transform the **IF** on the left into the **IF** on the right, we use test reversal. First, we change <test> to its opposite; then we switch the **do-nothing** instruction into the **ELSE** clause and bring <instruction> into the **THEN** clause. By the previous discussion of test reversal, execution equivalence is preserved. Finally, the new **ELSE** clause (which contains the **do-nothing** instruction) can be removed, resulting in the simpler **IF/THEN** instruction on the right.

The second transformation we discuss is bottom factoring. Bottom factoring is illustrated below, where we will show that the **IF/THEN/ELSE** instruction on the left is execution equivalent to the program fragment on the right. We have kept the bracketed words in these instructions because their exact replacements do not affect this transformation.

```
IF  <test> THEN             IF <test> THEN
    BEGIN                       <instruction-1>
        <instruction-1>;    ELSE    <instruction-2>;
        <instruction-3>         <instruction-3>
    END
ELSE
    BEGIN
        <instruction-2>;
        <instruction-3>
    END
```

In the program fragment on the right, we have *factored* <instruction-3> out of the bottom of each clause in the **IF**. (After factoring, we can remove both redundant **BEGIN/END** blocks.) We justify the correctness of this transformation as follows: If <test> is true, the instruction on the left has Karel execute <instruction-1> directly followed by <instruction-3>. In the program fragment on the right, if <test> is true, Karel executes <instruction-1> and then, having finished the **IF**, Karel executes <instruction-3>. Thus, when <test> is true, these forms are execution equivalent. A similar argument holds between the left and right fragments whenever <test> is false.

In summary, <instruction-3> is executed in the **IF** on the left regardless of whether <test> is true or false. Thus, we might as well remove it from each clause and put it directly after the entire **IF/THEN/ELSE** instruction. Moreover, if the bottoms of each clause were larger, but still identical, we could bottom factor all the common instructions and still preserve execution equivalence. Think of this process as bottom factoring one instruction at a time until all common instructions have been factored. Since execution equivalence is preserved during each factoring step, the resulting program fragment is execution equivalent to the original instruction.

The third transformation we discuss in this section is top factoring. Although this transformation may seem as simple and easy to use as bottom factoring, we will see that not all instructions can be top factored successfully. We divide our discussion of this transformation into three parts. First, we examine an instruction that can safely be top factored. Then we show an instruction that cannot be top factored successfully. Finally, we state a general rule that tells us which IF instructions can safely be top factored.

Top factoring can safely be used in the following example to convert the instruction on the left into the simpler program fragment on the right. These two forms can be shown to be execution equivalent by a justification similar to the one used in our discussion of bottom factoring.

```
IF  facing-north  THEN        move;
    BEGIN                     IF facing-north  THEN
    move;                         turnleft
    turnleft                  ELSE  turnright
    END
ELSE
    BEGIN
    move;
    turnright
    END
```

In the next example, we have incorrectly used the top factoring transformation. We will discover that the program fragment on the right is not execution equivalent to the instruction on the left.

```
IF  next-to-a-beeper  THEN      move;
    BEGIN                       IF next-to-a-beeper THEN
    move;                           turnleft
    turnleft                    ELSE  turnright
    END
ELSE
    BEGIN
    move;
    turnright
    END
```

To show that these forms execute differently, let's assume that Karel is on a corner containing one beeper and that the corner in front of the robot is barren. If Karel executes the instruction on the left, the robot will first find that it is next to a beeper and then will execute the THEN clause of the IF by moving forward and turning to its left. The program fragment on the right will first move Karel forward to the next corner and then will instruct it to test for a beeper. Since this new corner does not contain a beeper, Karel will execute the ELSE clause of the

IF, which causes the robot to turn to its right. Thus, top factoring in this example does not preserve execution equivalence.

Why can we correctly use top factoring in the first example but not in the second? The first instruction can be top factored safely because the test that determines which way Karel is facing is not changed by having it move forward. Therefore, whether or not Karel moves first, the evaluation of the test will remain unchanged. In the second example, however, the **move** changes the corner on which Karel checks for a beeper, so the robot is not performing the test under the same conditions. The general rule is that we may top factor an instruction only when the conditions under which the test is performed do not change between the original and factored versions of the instruction.

The fourth and final transformation is used to remove redundant tests in nested **IF** instructions. We call this transformation redundant-test-factoring and show one application of this rule.

```
IF  facing-west  THEN        IF  facing-west  THEN
  BEGIN                        BEGIN
    move;                        move;
    IF facing-west  THEN         turnleft
      turnleft                 END
  END
```

In the instruction on the left, there is no need for the nested **IF** instruction to recheck the condition **facing-west**. The **THEN** clause of the outer **IF** is executed only if Karel is facing west, and the **move** inside the **THEN** clause does not change the direction that Karel is facing. Therefore, **facing-west** is always true when Karel executes this nested **IF** instruction. This argument shows that Karel always executes the **THEN** clause of this nested **IF**. So, the entire nested **IF** instruction can be replaced by **turnleft**, as has been done in the instruction on the right. Once again, this transformation preserves execution equivalence. A similar transformation applies whenever we look for a redundant test in an **ELSE** clause. Remember, however, that in an **ELSE** clause <test> is false.

This transformation is also a bit more subtle than bottom factoring, and we must be careful when trying to use it. The potential difficulty is that intervening instructions might change Karel's position in an unknown way. For example, if instead of the **move** instruction we had written a **turn-around-if-next-to-beeper** instruction, we could not have used redundant-test-factoring. In this case, we cannot be sure whether Karel would be facing west or east when it had to execute the nested **IF**.

These four transformations can help us make our programs smaller, simpler, more logical, and—most important—more readable.

4.9 THE DANGLING **ELSE**

This section examines a syntactic anomaly of nested **IF** instructions. Look at the following two nested **IF**'s, and carefully study how each is boxed. We have kept the bracketed words in these instructions because their exact replacements do not affect our discussion.

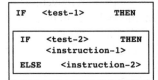

The difference between these two instructions is the boxing of the **ELSE** clause. In the first instruction, the **ELSE** is boxed with the nested **IF**, but in the second the **ELSE** is boxed with the outer **IF**. These are obviously two different instructions, yet Karel cannot tell them apart. To prove this, ignore the boxing and read each of the instructions. Both contain exactly the same words in exactly the same order.

We are therefore faced with two questions: First, if Karel reads this instruction, which way would the robot box it? Second, if we want the instruction boxed the other way, how would we tell Karel to do so? This anomaly is known in programming jargon as the dangling **ELSE** problem.

The first question is answered by introducing a new grammar rule. This rule states that whenever Karel reads an **ELSE** clause, the robot boxes it with the most recently read **IF** instruction of which it can be a part. Therefore, if Karel reads the preceding instruction, Karel boxes it like the previous boxing on the left.

We next show two related solutions to the second question. Karel interprets each of the following two instructions in a manner similar to the previous boxing on the right.

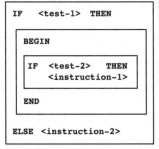
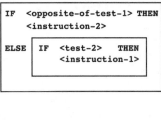

In the example on the left, we use a **BEGIN/END** block to inform Karel that the nested **IF** instruction is of the **IF/THEN** type. When Karel boxes this block, the **END** reserved word forces the robot to conclude that it has seen the entire nested **IF** instruction. Karel must treat the **BEGIN/END** block as a single instruction and must completely box all instructions within this block before reaching the **END** delimiter. Thus, when Karel finally reads the **ELSE**, there is only one **IF** instruction with which to match it.

We do not have to stop here. Now that we have the instruction on the left, we can simplify it by using test reversal. To perform test reversal, we replace `<test-1>` by its opposite and switch the **THEN** and **ELSE** clauses. Now the **BEGIN/END** block in the **ELSE** clause is redundant, so it can be removed. These two steps result in the instruction on the right, which allows Karel to match the **ELSE** with the outer **IF** unambiguously.

4.10   PROBLEM SET

The problems in this section require use of the `IF` instruction in its two forms. Try using stepwise refinement on these problems, but no matter what method you use to obtain a solution, write a clear and understandable program. Keep the nesting level small for those problems requiring nested `IF` instructions. Use proper punctuation and grammar, especially within the **THEN** and **ELSE** clauses of the `IF` instructions. Carefully simulate each definition and program that you write to ensure that there are no execution or intent errors.

1. Define `face-south`, a new instruction that is executed by facing Karel south regardless of the direction the robot is initially facing. First, do this without using `face-north` as a known instruction. Next, write `face-south` assuming that the instruction `face-north` has already been defined. This second definition should be much simpler, and given that `face-north` is correct, it should be easy to convince anyone of the correctness of `face-south`.

2. Look at the following instruction. Is there a simpler, execution equivalent instruction? If so, write it down; if not, explain why. *Hint:* A simplifying transformation for the `IF` may prove useful. Common sense also helps.

    ```
    IF not-next-to-a-beeper   THEN
            move
    ELSE   move
    ```

3. Assume that Karel is on a corner with either one or two beepers. Write a new instruction that commands the robot to face north if it is started on a corner with one beeper and to face south if it is started on a corner with two beepers. Besides facing the robot in the required direction, after Karel has executed this instruction there must be no beepers left on the corner. Name this instruction `find-next-direction`.

4. Write another version of `find-next-direction` (see the previous problem). In this version Karel must eventually face the same directions, but the robot must also leave the same number of beepers on the corner as were there originally.

5. Write an instruction that turns Karel off if the robot is completely surrounded by walls, unable to move in any direction. If Karel is not completely surrounded, it should execute this instruction by leaving itself turned on and by remaining on the same corner, facing the same direction in which it started. Name this instruction `turnoff-if-surrounded`. *Hint:* To write this instruction correctly, you will need to include a `turnoff` inside it. This combination is perfectly legal, but it is the first time that you will have to use a `turnoff` instruction outside of the **BEGINNING-OF-EXECUTION/END-OF-EXECUTION** block.

6. Program Karel to run a mile-long steeplechase. The steeplechase course is similar to the hurdle race, but here the barriers can be one, two, or three blocks high. Figure 4–5 shows one sample initial situation, where Karel's final situation and path are indicated on the right.

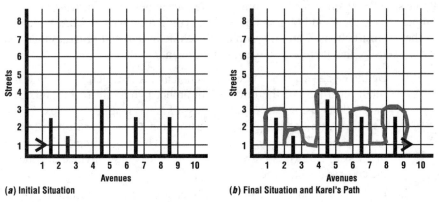

(*a*) Initial Situation   (*b*) Final Situation and Karel's Path

Figure 4–5   A Steeplechase Race Task

7. Rewrite and box the following new instruction, taking care to interpret all of Karel's grammar rules correctly. This instruction uses nested **IF**'s to face Karel toward the east; verify that it is correct by simulation. *Hint:* When trying to box this instruction, put yourself in Karel's place and ignore the instruction indentation. One way of doing this is to have someone read you the instruction. While they are reading the instruction, you should box it; after all, this is exactly what Karel does.

```
DEFINE-NEW-INSTRUCTION  face-east  AS
BEGIN
   IF not-facing-east  THEN
      IF  facing-west  THEN
         BEGIN
            turnleft;
            turnleft
         END
   ELSE
      IF  facing-north THEN
         turnright
      ELSE    turnleft
END;
```

8. The current version of **mystery-instruction** is syntactically correct but very difficult to read. Simplify it by using the **IF** transformations.

```
DEFINE-NEW-INSTRUCTION   mystery-instruction   AS
BEGIN
  IF facing-west   THEN
    BEGIN
      move;
      turnright;
      IF  facing-north   THEN
        move;
      turn-around
    END
  ELSE
    BEGIN
      move;
      turnleft;
      move;
      turn-around
    END
END;
```

9. Write an instruction named `follow-wall-right`, assuming that whenever Karel executes this instruction there is a wall directly to the right. Figure 4–6 shows all four of the different position changes that Karel must be able to make. This instruction is the cornerstone for a program that directs Karel to escape from a maze. (This maze-escape problem is presented in Problem 5.9–16.)

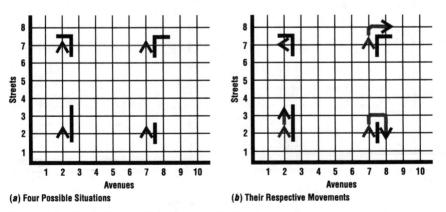

(a) Four Possible Situations   (b) Their Respective Movements

Figure 4–6   The `follow-wall-right` Specification

10. Program Karel to run a mile-long steeplechase where the steeples are made from beepers instead of wall segments. Karel must jump the steeples in this race by picking the beepers that make up the steeples. Each steeple is made from beepers that are positioned in columns that

are one, two, or three blocks long. Corners have either zero or one beeper. There are no gaps in any of the steeples. Figure 4–7 shows one sample initial situation.

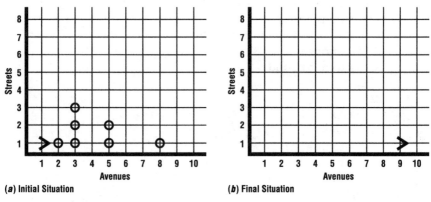

(*a*) Initial Situation   (*b*) Final Situation

Figure 4–7   A Different Steeplechase

11. Karel has been hired to carpet some "small rooms" along a one-mile section of its world. A "small room" is a corner that has a wall segment immediately to the west, north, and east. The door is to the south. Karel is to put a single beeper in only the "small rooms" and on no other corners. Figure 4–8 shows one set of initial and final situations. You may assume that Karel has exactly eight beepers in its beeper-bag.

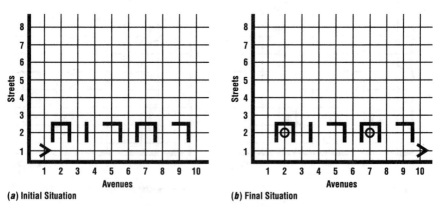

(*a*) Initial Situation   (*b*) Final Situation

Figure 4–8   Carpeting Some Small Rooms

12.   Karel did so well on the job in Problem 4.10–11 that the robot has been hired for a more complex carpeting task. The area to be carpeted is still one mile long. The rooms are now one, two, or three blocks long. The room must have continuous walls on its west and east side and at its northern end. If any walls are missing, the area must not be carpeted. Karel must also not reuse beepers. This means that once a beeper has been put down, it must not be picked up. Figure 4–9 shows one set of initial and final situations. You may assume that Karel has exactly 24 beepers in its beeper-bag.

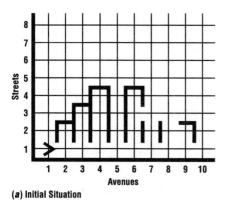
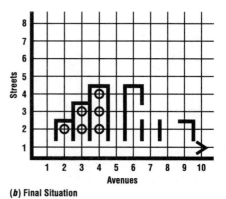

(a) Initial Situation   (b) Final Situation

Figure 4–9   More Complex Carpet Laying

5 INSTRUCTIONS THAT REPEAT

This chapter completes our discussion of the instructions that are built into Karel's vocabulary. The two new instructions we will learn are **ITERATE** and **WHILE**. Both of these instructions can repeatedly execute any instruction that Karel understands, including nested **ITERATE** and **WHILE** instructions. These additions greatly enhance the conciseness and power of the robot programming language. In Section 5.7 we will construct a complex, room-escaping robot program by using stepwise refinement and all the instructions we have learned.

Since we are becoming experienced robot programmers, we will use an abbreviated view of Karel's world for some of the figures. To reduce visual clutter, the street and avenue labels and, in some instances, the southern or western boundary walls will not be shown.

5.1 THE ITERATE INSTRUCTION

When we program Karel, it is sometimes necessary to have the robot repeat an instruction a certain number of times. We previously handled this problem by writing the instruction as many times as needed. The **ITERATE** instruction provides us with a mechanism that allows Karel to repeat another instruction a specified number of times. It has the following general form.

```
ITERATE <positive-number> TIMES
    <instruction>
```

This instruction introduces the reserved words **ITERATE** and **TIMES**. The bracketed word <**positive-number**> tells Karel how many times to execute the instruction that replaces < **instruction**>. We refer to < **instruction**> as the body of the **ITERATE** instruction, and we will also use the term **ITERATE** loop to suggest verbally that this instruction loops back and executes its body. Our first example of an **ITERATE** loop is another definition of **turnright**.

```
DEFINE-NEW-INSTRUCTION turnright AS
BEGIN
    ITERATE 3 TIMES
    turnleft
END;
```

As a second example, we rewrite the **harvest-1-row** instruction that was written in Section 3.8.1. This definition originally comprised nine primitive instructions, but by using **ITERATE** we can define the instruction more concisely. With this new, more general version of **harvest-1-row**, we can now easily increase or decrease the number of beepers harvested per row; all we need to change is <**positive-number**> in the **ITERATE** instruction.

```
DEFINE-NEW-INSTRUCTION harvest-1-row AS
BEGIN
    pickbeeper;
    ITERATE 4 TIMES
        BEGIN
            move;
            pickbeeper
        END
END;
```

Finally, we show one **ITERATE** instruction nested within another. Carefully observe the way this instruction is boxed, for this is a strong clue to how Karel executes it.

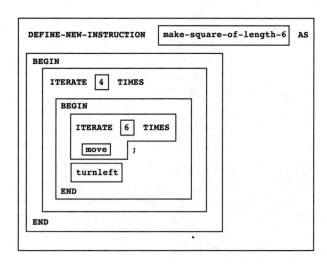

If we assume no intervening walls, this instruction moves Karel around the perimeter of a square whose sides are six blocks long. The outer **ITERATE** instruction loops a total of four times, once for each side of the square. Each time the outer **ITERATE** loop's body is executed, Karel executes two instructions. First, the robot executes the nested **ITERATE**, which moves Karel six blocks. Then Karel executes the **turnleft**, which prepares it to trace the next side. Thus, Karel executes a total of twenty-four moves and four left turns, which are arranged in an order that makes it travel in a square.

5.2   THE **WHILE** INSTRUCTION

In this section we explain the **WHILE** instruction and analyze many of its interesting properties. It is the most powerful instruction that is built into Karel's vocabulary.

5.2.1   Why **WHILE** Is Needed

To motivate the need for a **WHILE** instruction, we look at what should be a simple programming task. Assume that Karel is initially facing east on some street and that somewhere east of the robot on that same street is a beeper. Karel's task is to move forward until it is on the same corner as the beeper and then to pick it up. Despite this simple description, the program is impossible to write with our current repertoire of instructions. Two attempts at solving this problem might be written as follows.

```
IF not-next-to-a-beeper  THEN          ITERATE ? TIMES
    move;                                  move;
IF not-next-to-a-beeper  THEN          pickbeeper
    move;
        .
        .
        .
IF not-next-to-a-beeper  THEN
    move;
pickbeeper
```

We can interpret what is meant by these instructions, but Karel understands neither "..." nor "?". The difficulty is that we do not know in advance how many **move** instructions Karel must execute before it arrives at the same corner as the beeper; we do not even have a guaranteed upper limit! The beeper may be on Karel's starting street corner, or it may be a million blocks away. Karel must be able to accomplish this task without knowing in advance the number of corners that it will pass before reaching the beeper. We must program Karel to execute **move** instructions repeatedly, until the robot senses that it is next to the beeper. What we need is an instruction that combines the repetition ability of the **ITERATE** instruction with the testing ability of the **IF** instruction.

5.2.2   The Form of the WHILE Instruction

The **WHILE** instruction commands Karel to repeat another instruction as long as some test remains true. The **WHILE** instruction is executed somewhat similarly to an **IF/THEN** instruction, except that the **WHILE** instruction repeatedly executes itself as long as <test> is true. The general form of the **WHILE** instruction is given as follows.

```
          WHILE <test> DO
            <instruction>
```

The new reserved word **WHILE** starts this instruction, and the reserved word **DO** separates <test> from the body of the **WHILE** loop. The conditions that can replace <test> are the same ones that are used in the **IF** instructions.

Karel executes a **WHILE** loop by first checking <test> in its current situation. If <test> is true, Karel executes <instruction> and then re-executes the entire **WHILE** loop. If <test> is false, Karel is finished with the **WHILE** instruction, and the robot continues by executing the instructions following the entire **WHILE** loop. Here is a sample **WHILE** instruction, which solves the problem that began this discussion.

```
     DEFINE-NEW-INSTRUCTION go-to-beeper AS
     BEGIN
        WHILE not-next-to-a-beeper DO
          move
     END;
```

This instruction moves Karel forward as long as **not-next-to-a-beeper** is true. When Karel is finally next to a beeper, it finishes executing the **WHILE** loop. The following instruction is another simple example of a **WHILE** loop, and we will examine its behavior in detail.

```
     DEFINE-NEW-INSTRUCTION clear-corner-of-beepers AS
     BEGIN
        WHILE next-to-a-beeper DO
          pickbeeper
     END;
```

This instruction commands Karel to pick up all the beepers on a corner. Let's simulate Karel's execution of this instruction on a corner containing two beepers. Karel first determines whether **next-to-a-beeper** is true or false. Finding the test true, it executes the body of the **WHILE** loop, which is the **pickbeeper** instruction. Then Karel re-executes the entire **WHILE** loop. The robot finds <test> is true (one beeper is still left) and executes the body of the **WHILE** loop. After picking up the second beeper, Karel re-executes the entire **WHILE** instruction. Although we know that there are no beepers remaining, Karel is unaware of this fact until it re-checks the **WHILE** loop test. Now Karel re-checks the test and discovers that **next-to-a-beeper** is false, so the robot is finished executing the **WHILE** loop. Because the entire definition consists of one **WHILE** loop, Karel is finished executing **clear-corner-of-beepers**. It appears that no matter how many beepers are initially on the corner, Karel will eventually pick them all up when this instruction is executed.

What happens if Karel executes **clear-corner-of-beepers** on a corner that has no beepers? In this special situation, <test> is false the first time that the **WHILE** instruction is executed, so the loop body is not executed at all. Therefore, Karel also handles this situation correctly. The key fact to remember about a **WHILE** instruction is that until Karel discovers that <test> has become false— and it may be false the first time—Karel repeatedly checks <test> and executes the loop's body.

5.2.3   Building a WHILE Loop—The Four-Step Process

In the previous chapter on **IF**'s we discussed the problems novice programmers frequently face when they are introduced to a new programming construct. We are in a similar situation with the **WHILE** loop. We have seen the form of a **WHILE** loop, looked at an example, and traced the execution of the example. Before using a **WHILE** loop in a robot program, it would be helpful to have a framework for thinking about the **WHILE** loop.

We should consider using a **WHILE** loop only when Karel must do something an unknown number of times. If we are faced with such a situation, we can build our **WHILE** loop by following the four-step process described next. To illustrate these steps, we will again use the problem of having Karel pick all beepers from a corner without knowing the initial number of beepers on the corner.

Step 1:   Identify the one test that must be true when Karel is finished with the loop.

In the above problem, Karel must pick all beepers on the corner. If we consider only tests that involve beepers, we can choose among four: **any-beepers-in-beeper-bag**, **no-beepers-in-beeper-bag**, **next-to-a-beeper**, and **not-next-to-a-beeper**. Which one is the test we want? When Karel is finished, there should be no beepers left on the corner, so the test we want to be true is **not-next-to-a-beeper**.

Step 2:   Use the opposite form of the test identified in step 1 as the loop <test>.

This step implies that we should use **next-to-a-beeper**. Does this make sense? The **WHILE** instruction continues to execute the loop body as long as the test is true and stops when it is false. As long as Karel is next to a beeper, it should pick them up. When it is done, there will be no beepers on the corner.

Step 3: Do whatever is required before or after the **WHILE** is executed to ensure we solve the given problem.

In this example, we have to do nothing before or after the loop. However, at times we may miss one iteration of the loop and have to "clean things up," which can be done either before or after the **WHILE**.

Step 4: Do the minimum that is needed to ensure that the test eventually evaluates to false so that the **WHILE** loop stops.

Something within the body of the loop must allow the test eventually to evaluate to false or the loop will run forever. This implies that there must be some instruction (or sequence of instructions) within the loop that is related to the test. In this problem, what must be done to bring us closer to the test being false? Since we are testing for **not-next-to-a-beeper**, we must pick one (and only one) beeper somewhere in the loop. We can argue that if Karel keeps picking one beeper, it must eventually pick all the beepers, leaving none on the corner. Why pick only one beeper during each iteration? Why not two or three? If there is only one beeper on the corner, and we instruct Karel to pick up more than one, an error shutoff will occur. Picking just one beeper during each iteration of the loop is the minimum needed to guarantee that all the beepers are picked up.

If we follow these four steps carefully, we reduce the chance of having intent errors and infinite repetition when we test our program.

5.2.4 A More Interesting Problem

Let's apply these four steps to a new problem. Karel is somewhere in the world facing south. One beeper is on each corner between Karel's current position and the southern boundary wall. There is no beeper on the corner on which it is currently standing. Write a new instruction, **clear-all-beepers-to-the-wall**, to pick all the beepers (Figure 5–1).

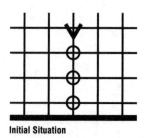

Initial Situation

Figure 5–1   Pick All Beepers

As before, let's ask ourselves some questions:

Question: What do we know about Karel's initial situation?

Answer: Karel is facing south.

Karel is an unknown distance from the southern boundary wall.

Each corner between Karel and the southern boundary wall has one beeper.

Question: Does any of this information provide insight toward a solution?

Answer: Karel can travel forward until it reaches the southern boundary wall. It can pick a beeper from each corner as it travels.

We have the beginnings of a plan. We continue the process.

Question: What Karel instruction can we use to keep Karel traveling southward until it reaches the southern boundary wall?

Answer: Since traveling to the southern boundary wall requires an unknown number of **move** instructions, we can use a **WHILE** loop.

Question: How do we actually use the **WHILE** loop?

Answer: We can use the four-step process as follows:

Step 1:   Identify the one test that must be true when Karel is finished with the loop. Karel will be at the southern boundary wall, so the test **front-is-blocked** will be true.

Step 2:   Use the opposite form of the test identified in step 1 as the loop <test>. The opposite form is **front-is-clear**.

Step 3:   Do whatever is required before or after the **WHILE** is executed to ensure we solve the given problem. Since Karel is already facing south, we do not have to do anything.

Step 4:   Do the minimum that is needed to ensure that the test eventually evaluates to false so that the **WHILE** loop stops. Karel must **move** forward one block within the loop body, but we must be careful here. Karel is not yet standing on a beeper, so it must **move** first before picking the beeper. We can use a single **pickbeeper** instruction because there is only one beeper on each corner.

Based on this discussion, we can write the following new instruction:

```
DEFINE-NEW-INSTRUCTION clear-all-beepers-to-the-wall AS
  BEGIN
    WHILE front-is-clear DO
      BEGIN
        move;
        pickbeeper
      END
  END;
```

Our work is not finished. We must carefully trace the execution before we certify it as correct. Can we test all possible situations in which Karel could start this task? No! We cannot test all possible situations, but we can test several and do a reasonable job of convincing ourselves that the instruction is correct. One method of informally reasoning about the instruction follows.

First: Show that the instruction works correctly when the initial situation results in the test being false. That would mean that the initial situation would look as depicted in Figure 5–2.

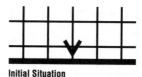

Initial Situation

Figure 5–2   The Same Task
Without Beepers

Second: Show that each time the loop body is executed, Karel's new situation is a simpler and similar version of the old situation. By simpler we mean that Karel now has less work to do before finishing the loop. By similar we mean that Karel's situation has not radically changed during its execution of the loop body. (In this example, a nonsimilar change could mean that Karel is facing a different direction.) If our new instruction is correct, we should see these changes in the following Karel world (Figure 5–3).

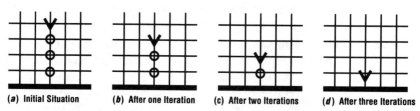

(*a*) Initial Situation   (*b*) After one Iteration   (c) After two Iterations   (*d*) After three Iterations

Figure 5–3   Tracing Karel's Progress Executing the Loop

After each iteration of the loop, the current corner should have no beepers. Take some time and trace the robot's execution of the loop and verify that it is correct.

5.3   ERRORS TO AVOID WITH WHILE LOOPS

The **WHILE** loop provides a powerful tool for our robot programs. Using it wisely, we can instruct Karel to solve some very complex problems. However, the sharper the ax, the deeper it can cut. With the power of the WHILE loop comes the potential for making some powerful mistakes. This section examines several typical errors that can be made when using the WHILE loop. If we are aware of these errors, we will have a better chance of avoiding them or, at least, an easier time identifying them for correction.

5.3.1   The Fence Post Problem

If we order six fence posts, how many sections of fence do we need? The obvious answer is six! But it is wrong. Think about it. (See Figure 5–4.)

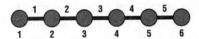

Figure 5–4   The Fence Post Problem

This figure should help us to understand why the correct answer is five. We can encounter the fence post problem when using the WHILE loop. Let's take the previous problem with a slight twist and put a beeper on Karel's starting corner. (See Figure 5–5.)

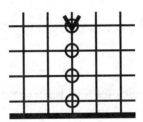

Figure 5–5   Initial Situation

Suppose we decide to solve this problem by reversing the order of the instructions in the original loop body and have Karel pick the beeper before moving:

```
DEFINE-NEW-INSTRUCTION clear-all-beepers-to-the-wall AS
   BEGIN
      WHILE front-is-clear DO
         BEGIN
            pickbeeper;
            move
         END
   END;
```

If we trace the instruction's execution carefully, we will discover that the loop still finishes—there is no error shutoff. However, the southernmost beeper is not picked. (See Figure 5–6.)

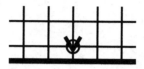

Figure 5–6 Final Situation

In this example the beepers were the fence posts, and the moves were the fence sections. The **WHILE** loop executes the same number of **pickbeeper** and **move** instructions. Consequently, one beeper will be left when the loop finishes. This is where step 3 in the four-step process comes in. We now have a situation where we must do something before or after the loop to make sure we solve the given problem. There are at least two ways to handle this problem. Here is one.

```
DEFINE-NEW-INSTRUCTION clear-all-beepers-to-the-wall AS
  BEGIN
    WHILE front-is-clear DO
      BEGIN
        pickbeeper;
        move
      END;
    pickbeeper
  END;
```

Our solution is simply to pick the final beeper after the **WHILE** loop stops executing. What is the other way to solve this fence post problem?

5.3.2 Infinite Execution

Having looked at step 3 in the four-step process, let's now focus our attention on step 4: do the minimum that is needed to ensure that the test eventually evaluates to false so that the **WHILE** loop stops. Sometimes we forget to include an instruction (or sequence of instructions), the execution of which allows the test eventually to become false. Here is an example:

```
WHILE facing-north DO
  BEGIN
    pickbeeper;
    move
  END
```

Look at this loop carefully. Is there any instruction within the loop body that will change Karel's direction? Neither **pickbeeper** nor **move** does so. The loop will iterate zero times if Karel is initially facing any direction other than north. Unfortunately, if Karel is facing north, we condemn the robot to walk forever (since the world is infinite to the north) or to execute an error shutoff if it arrives at a corner without a beeper. When we plan the body of the **WHILE** loop, we must be very careful to avoid the possibility of infinite repetition.

5.3.3   When the Test of a WHILE Is Checked

Section 5.2.2 explained how Karel executes a **WHILE** instruction, yet unless it is read carefully, it may be somewhat ambiguous. In this section we closely examine the execution of a **WHILE** instruction and explain a common misconception about when Karel checks <**test**>. Let's examine the following instruction carefully.

```
DEFINE-NEW-INSTRUCTION harvest-line AS
BEGIN
   WHILE next-to-a-beeper DO
      BEGIN
         pickbeeper;
         move
      END
END;
```

This instruction commands Karel to pick up a line of beepers. The robot finishes executing this instruction after moving one block beyond the final corner that has a beeper.

Let's simulate this new instruction in detail for a line of two beepers. Karel starts its task on the same corner as the first beeper. Karel executes the **WHILE** instruction and finds that the test is true, so it executes the body of the loop. The loop body instructs Karel to pick up the beeper and then move to the next corner. Now Karel re-executes the loop; the test is checked, and again Karel senses that it is next to a beeper. The robot picks up the second beeper and moves forward. Karel then executes the loop again. Now when the test is checked, the robot finds that its corner is beeperless, so it is finished executing the **WHILE** loop. The definition of **harvest-line** contains only one instruction—this **WHILE** loop—so **harvest-line** is also finished.

The point demonstrated here is that Karel checks <**test**> only before it executes the body of the loop. Karel is totally insensitive to <**test**> while executing instructions that are inside the loop body. A common misconception among novice programmers is that Karel checks <**test**> after each instruction is executed inside the loop body. This is an incorrect interpretation of when Karel checks <**test**>.

Let's see what would happen if Karel used the incorrect interpretation to execute the **harvest-line** instruction in the two-beeper situation. This interpretation would force Karel to finish the **WHILE** loop as soon as it was not next to a beeper. Karel would start by determining if it was next to a beeper. Finding the test true, Karel would execute the loop body. This is fine so far, but after executing the **pickbeeper**, Karel would not be next to a beeper anymore. So, according to this incorrect interpretation, Karel would now be finished with the loop and would be limited to picking up only one beeper regardless of the length of the beeper line.

5.4 NESTED WHILE LOOPS

We have already discussed nesting, or the placing of one instruction within a similar instruction. Nesting **WHILE** loops can be a very useful technique if done properly, and in this section we will look at both a good and a bad example of nesting.

5.4.1 A Good Example of Nesting

We will use a modification of a previous problem. Karel is somewhere in the world facing south. Between its current location and the southern boundary wall are beepers. We do not know how many beepers are on each corner. (Some corners may even have no beepers.) Write a new instruction that will direct Karel to pick all the beepers between its current location and the southern boundary wall (Figure 5–7).

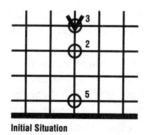

Initial Situation

Figure 5–7 A Problem to Move and Pick Beepers

We can use our question/answer format to plan a solution to this problem.

Question: What is the problem?

Answer: We must move Karel an unknown distance and have Karel pick an unknown number of beepers from each corner it passes.

Question: What does Karel have to do?

Answer: Karel must perform two tasks:

- First, Karel must walk an unknown distance to the southern wall.
- Second, Karel must pick all the beepers on each corner it encounters. There may be from zero to a very large number of beepers on each corner.

Let's concentrate on the first task and save the second task for later.

Question: What instruction can we use to keep Karel moving forward to the southern boundary wall?

Answer: Since this requires an unknown number of iterations of the **move** instruction, we can use the **WHILE** loop.

We can apply the four-step process for building **WHILE** loops and write the following code for Karel to test.

```
WHILE front-is-clear DO
  BEGIN
    move
  END
```

If Karel executes this instruction correctly, then our plan is on the right track. However, if Karel stops before arriving at the boundary wall or executes an error shutoff when it tries to move through the wall, we must re-analyze our plan. This instruction works properly, so we now consider the second task—Karel's picking of all beepers on each corner it encounters as it travels to the boundary wall.

Question: What instruction will allow Karel to pick all the beepers that might be on a corner?

Answer: Since this requires an unknown number of iterations of the pick-beeper instruction, we can use the **WHILE** instruction to do this task also.

We can apply the four-step process for building **WHILE** loops and write the following implementation.

```
WHILE next-to-a-beeper DO
  BEGIN
    pickbeeper
  END
```

We simulate this loop, and it appears to work. We now have to decide which loop to nest inside of which loop. Do we put the loop that moves Karel to the southern boundary wall inside the loop that picks beepers, or do we put the beeper-picking loop inside the loop that moves Karel to the wall?

Question: Can we interchange these two actions?

Answer: No, we cannot. Arriving at the wall should stop both Karel's mov-ing and picking. Running out of beepers on one corner should NOT stop Karel's moving to the wall. As we move to the wall, we can clean each corner of beepers if we nest the beeper-picking loop inside the loop that moves Karel to the wall.

Our new instruction definition will look like this.

```
DEFINE-NEW-INSTRUCTION clear-all-beepers-to-the-wall AS
  BEGIN
    WHILE front-is-clear DO
      BEGIN
        WHILE next-to-a-beeper DO
          pickbeeper;
        move
      END
  END;
```

When we nest **WHILE** loops, we must be very sure that the execution of the nested loop (or inner loop) does not interfere with the test condition of the outer loop. In this problem the inner loop is responsible for picking beepers, and the outer loop is responsible for moving the robot. Since these two activities do not affect each other, the nesting seems to be correct.

We are not done. We must now test this new instruction. Take some time and trace Karel's execution of it using the initial situation shown in Figure 5–7. As much as we would like to believe it is correct, it isn't. We appear to have forgotten the fence post discussion of Section 5.3.1. The way we have written the new instruction, the last corner will not be cleared of beepers; this last corner is our forgotten fence post. To ensure that the last corner is cleared of beepers, we must make one more modification.

```
DEFINE-NEW-INSTRUCTION clear-all-beepers-to-the-wall AS
  BEGIN
    WHILE front-is-clear DO
      BEGIN
        WHILE next-to-a-beeper DO
          pickbeeper;
        move
      END;
    WHILE next-to-a-beeper DO
      pickbeeper
  END;
```

This modification, a third loop that is outside of the nested loops, will clear the last corner of beepers.

One note is in order here about the overall design of our new instruction. As a rule, we prefer to perform only one task (e.g., moving to a wall) in a new instruction and to move secondary tasks (e.g., picking the beepers) into a different new instruction. We believe the following represents a better programming style for the previous new instruction.

```
DEFINE-NEW-INSTRUCTION clear-beepers-this-corner AS
  BEGIN
    WHILE next-to-a-beeper DO
      pickbeeper
  END;


DEFINE-NEW-INSTRUCTION clear-all-beepers-to-the-wall AS
  BEGIN
    WHILE front-is-clear DO
      BEGIN
        clear-beepers-this-corner;
        move
      END;
    clear-beepers-this-corner
  END;
```

This programming style is easier to read, and, if we suddenly find that clearing the beepers requires a different strategy, we only have to make a change in one place, **clear-beepers-this-corner**.

5.4.2   A Bad Example of Nesting

Karel is facing south in the northwest corner of a room that has no doors or windows. Somewhere in the room, next to a wall, is a single beeper. Instruct Karel to find the beeper by writing the new instruction, **find-beeper**. (See Figure 5–8.)

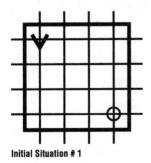

Initial Situation # 1

Figure 5–8   Initial Situation

We begin with our usual question/answer planning.

Question: What is the problem?

Answer: We must instruct Karel to find a beeper that is somewhere in the room next to the wall. We do not know how far away it is, and we do not know how big the room is.

Question: What instruction can we use to move Karel to the beeper?

Answer: Since the distance Karel must travel is unknown, we can use a WHILE loop.

Using the four-step process to build a WHILE loop, we develop the following new instruction.

```
DEFINE-NEW-INSTRUCTION find-beeper AS
  BEGIN
    WHILE not-next-to-a-beeper DO
      BEGIN
        move
      END
  END;
```

If we analyze this new instruction carefully, we find, as shown in Figure 5–9, that Karel executes an error shutoff when it arrives at the southern wall.

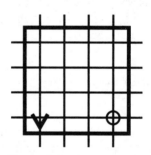

Figure 5–9 Karel Executes an Error Shutoff

Question: What happened?

Answer: We forgot about turning Karel at the corners.

Question: How can we fix this problem?

Answer: Let's walk Karel forward until it detects a wall.

Question: What instruction can we use to do this?

Answer: Since the distance Karel must travel is unknown, we can use a WHILE loop.

Again we use the four-step process to build a nested **WHILE** loop and to develop the following new instruction.

```
DEFINE-NEW-INSTRUCTION find-beeper AS
  BEGIN
    WHILE not-next-to-a-beeper DO
      BEGIN
        WHILE front-is-clear DO
          BEGIN
            move
          END;
        turnleft
      END
  END;
```

We must test this instruction to see if it works. Since this problem is somewhat involved, we should use several different initial situations. Will the situations shown in Figure 5–10 be sufficient to test our code completely?

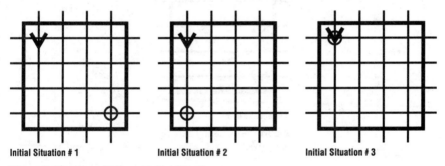

Initial Situation # 1   Initial Situation # 2   Initial Situation # 3

Figure 5–10   Three Different Initial Situations

If we trace our program using these situations, it appears that our instruction is correct. However, does the original problem statement guarantee that the beeper will always be in a corner? It does not. The original problem statement says that the beeper is somewhere next to a wall. Each of our three test situations puts the beeper in a corner. We should try an initial situation such as the one shown in Figure 5–11.

Let's see what happens here: Karel makes the outer test, **not-next-to-a-beeper**, and it is true, so it begins to execute the outer loop body. Karel makes the inner test, **front-is-clear**, which is true; thus, Karel moves forward one block, coming to rest on the corner with the beeper. What happens now? Karel remains focused on the inner loop. It has not forgotten about the outer loop, but its focus is restricted to the inner loop until the inner loop stops execution. Karel is required to make the inner test, **front-is-clear**, which is true, and moves one block forward away from the beeper. This is now Karel's situation (Figure 5–12).

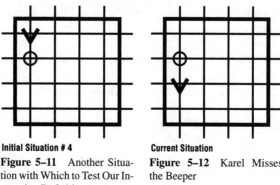

Initial Situation # 4

Figure 5–11   Another Situation with Which to Test Our Instruction Definition

Current Situation

Figure 5–12   Karel Misses the Beeper

Karel remains focused on the inner loop and makes the inner test again. It is true, and so Karel executes the move and is now in the situation shown in Figure 5–13:

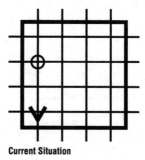

Current Situation

Figure 5–13   Karel Arrives at the Wall

The inner test is false, so Karel ceases execution of the inner loop, executes the **turnleft**, and is done with the first iteration of the outer loop. Now Karel makes the outer test, **not-next-to-a-beeper**, which is true. Karel has no memory of once standing next to a beeper; consequently, Karel will continue to walk around this room and keep going and going and going. . . . Our instruction will execute infinitely in this case!

There must be something wrong with our initial reasoning. Let's look at the initial planning segment.

Question: *What is the problem?*

Answer: *We must instruct Karel to find a beeper that is somewhere in the room next to the wall. We do not know how far away it is, and we do not know how big the room is.*

Question: *What instruction can we use to move Karel to the beeper?*

Answer: *Since the distance Karel must travel is unknown, we can use a* **WHILE** *loop.*

We then found that Karel performed an error shutoff because we instructed Karel to move forward when the front was blocked by a wall. Our next planning segment appears below.

Question: *What happened?*

Answer: *We forgot about turning Karel at the corners.*

Question: *How can we fix this problem?*

Answer: *Let's walk Karel forward until it detects a wall.*

Question: *What instruction can we use to do this?*

Answer: *Since the distance Karel must travel is unknown, we can use a* WHILE *loop.*

This is where our plan began to go wrong. We decided to walk Karel forward until the front was blocked. We reasoned that we could use a WHILE loop to move Karel forward, and that was the mistake. If the robot moves more than one block forward without allowing the test of the outer WHILE loop to be checked, it will violate step 4 of the four-step process—Do whatever is needed to ensure the loop stops. Karel should only move one block forward within the outer WHILE loop. We should not use an inner WHILE loop to move Karel toward the wall! The reason is that Karel's execution of the inner WHILE loop can cause the outer WHILE loop never to stop. Both the outer and inner WHILE loops require Karel to execute the **move** instruction to eventually terminate both loops. Unless both tests, **not-next-to-a-beeper** and **front-is-clear**, are false at the exact same time, the outer loop will never stop. We must discard the inner WHILE loop and find a different way to keep Karel from trying to move through the wall.

Question: How can we move Karel forward without the WHILE loop?

Answer: Karel should only move forward one block inside the WHILE loop, so we must use an **IF/THEN/ELSE** statement to check for a wall. Karel will move when the front is clear and turn left when a wall is present.

Following our new reasoning, we have a new instruction.

```
DEFINE-NEW-INSTRUCTION find-beeper AS
   BEGIN
      WHILE not-next-to-a-beeper DO
         BEGIN
            IF front-is-clear THEN
               move
            ELSE turnleft
         END
   END;
```

Nesting WHILE loops is a powerful programming idea, but with this increased power comes the increased need for very careful planning and analysis.

5.5 WHILE AND IF INSTRUCTIONS

Novice programmers frequently use WHILE and IF instructions in a conflicting, unnecessary, or redundant manner. Examine the following program fragments to find improperly used tests.

```
IF facing-south THEN
    WHILE not-facing-south DO
        turnleft
```

In this fragment there are conflicting tests. When the IF's test is true, the WHILE's test must be false. This fragment will do nothing.
Let's try another one.

```
WHILE front-is-blocked DO
    IF front-is-clear THEN
        move
    ELSE turnleft
```

In this fragment there is an unnecessary test. When the WHILE's test is true, the IF's test must be false, so the ELSE is the only part of the loop body that is ever executed.
Here is one more fragment.

```
WHILE next-to-a-beeper DO
    IF next-to-a-beeper THEN
        pickbeeper
```

In this fragment there are redundant tests. The WHILE's test is the same as the IF's test. When the WHILE's test is true, so is the IF's.

Problems such as these usually enter our programs when we attempt to fix execution or intent errors. We sometimes get so involved in the details of our program that we forget to take a step back and look at the overall picture. Therefore, it is often very helpful to take a break and come back to the program with fresh eyes.

5.6 REASONING ABOUT LOOPS

In Section 5.2.3 we discussed the four-step process for building a WHILE loop.

1. Identify the one test that must be true when Karel is finished with the loop.
2. Use the opposite form of the test identified in step 1 as the loop <test>.
3. Do whatever is required before or after the WHILE is executed to ensure we solve the given problem.
4. Do the minimum that is needed to ensure that the test eventually evaluates to false so that the WHILE loop stops.

We also presented an informal way to reason about the correctness of WHILE loops.

1.   Show that the instruction works correctly when the initial situation results in the test being false.

2.   Show that each time the loop body is executed, Karel's new situation is a simpler and similar version of the old situation.

We'd like to spend a little more time discussing this last concept of correctness. Remember that Karel will do exactly what it is told and only what it is told. It is up to us to make sure that Karel is provided with a correct way to solve a given problem. At the same time, we need a way to "prove" (in some sense) that our solution is correct. Because we cannot simulate every possible situation, we need to think through our solution in a formal way to verify that it does what it is supposed to do.

In order to reason about WHILE loops, we will need to understand a key concept called a loop invariant. A loop invariant is an assertion (something that can be proven true or false) that is true after each iteration of the loop. For our purposes, loop invariants will be assertions about Karel's world. In particular, the items that we need to be concerned about after ONE iteration are the following:

- How has Karel's direction changed, if at all?
- How has Karel's relative position in the world changed, if at all? (This may involve thinking about wall segments as well.)
- How has the number of beepers in Karel's beeper-bag changed, if at all?
- How has the number of beepers in the world changed, if at all?

Let's look at these items using the example given in Section 5.2.4, clear-all-beepers-to-the-wall. After one iteration of the following loop,

```
WHILE front-is-clear DO
   BEGIN
      move;
      pickbeeper
   END
```

what can we say (assert) with regard to the items mentioned above? We can assert the following:

- Karel's direction is unchanged.
- Karel's position has been advanced forward one corner.
- That corner has one less beeper.
- Karel's beeper-bag has one more beeper.

Which of these statements are "interesting?" By "interesting" we mean which item is important in terms of the problem being solved? Since we're removing beepers, we're interested in the second and third assertions. A loop invariant captures the "interesting" change during one iteration of the loop. Thus, for this problem, the loop invariant is that Karel has advanced one corner and removed one beeper from that corner.

What else have we learned? Let's look at our loop test, `front-is-clear`. When the loop ends, it will be false; thus, the front will be blocked. So we know that when the loop terminates, Karel has removed one beeper from each corner it has passed and Karel's front is now blocked. We have learned that, as long as each corner had one beeper on it, our loop must have solved the problem of picking up beepers to the wall.

Let's look at the fence post problem presented in Section 5.3.1. What is the loop invariant for the first attempt at solving that problem? Here's the loop:

```
WHILE front-is-clear DO
    BEGIN
    pickbeeper;
    move
    END
```

What can we assert about this loop?

• Karel's direction is unchanged.
• Karel's position has been advanced forward one corner.
• The previous corner has one less beeper.
• Karel's beeper-bag has one more beeper.

What do we know about Karel and the world when the loop finishes? We know that any previous corners have had one beeper removed from them, and this is the loop invariant.

What about Karel's current corner? Since the loop invariant only mentions previous corners, we know nothing about the corner on which Karel is standing when the loop terminates—it may have a beeper, it may not. How we choose to remedy this situation is up to us, but at least in reasoning about the loop we have become aware of a potential problem with our loop—the fence post problem.

Loop invariants can be powerful tools in aiding our understanding of how a loop is operating and what it will cause Karel to do. The key lies in determining how executing the loop changes the state of the world during each iteration and in capturing that change as succinctly as possible. Once we've discovered the loop invariant, we can use it and the loop's termination condition to decide whether the loop solves the problem. If not, we must look back over the steps for constructing a **WHILE** loop to see where we might have gone wrong.

Another use of loop invariants is to help us determine what instructions we want to use in the loop body. So far we've used the loop invariant as an after-the-fact device, to verify that a loop we've written solves a specific problem. If we determine what we want the invariant to be before we write the body of the loop, it can help decide what the body should be. As an example, consider the following problem: Karel is searching for a beeper that is an unknown distance directly in front of it, and there may be some one-block-high wall segments in the way.

What do we want to be true when the loop terminates? Since Karel is looking for a beeper, we want Karel to be on a beeper. Thus, our test is `not-next-to-a-beeper`. What do we want to be the invariant? Karel must move one (and only one) block in the initial direction during each iteration of the loop to ensure that each corner is examined. Our first pass at a loop might look like this:

```
WHILE not-next-to-a-beeper DO
    BEGIN
        move
    END
```

Unfortunately, this loop will cause an error shutoff if we happen to run into one of those intervening wall segments before reaching the beeper. How can we maintain our invariant and still avoid the wall segment? A little insight might suggest the following modification:

```
WHILE not-next-to-a-beeper DO
    BEGIN
        IF front-is-clear THEN
            move
        ELSE
            avoid-wall
    END
```

where `avoid-wall` is defined as

```
DEFINE-NEW-INSTRUCTION avoid-wall AS
    BEGIN
        turnleft;
        move;
        turnright;
        move;
        turnright;
        move;
        turnleft
    END;
```

In defining `avoid-wall`, we must keep the loop invariant in mind. We want to make progress toward our goal, but as little progress as possible so that we don't accidentally miss something. We should spend some time convincing ourselves that this loop does indeed maintain the initial invariant: that Karel moves one (and only one) block in the initial direction during each iteration of the loop. We should also convince ourselves that this loop does solve the problem.

5.7 A LARGE PROGRAM WRITTEN BY STEPWISE REFINEMENT

In this section we will write a complex program by using stepwise refinement. The program instructs Karel to escape from any rectangular room that has an open doorway exactly one block wide. After escaping from the room, the program commands Karel to turn itself off.

Instead of deftly avoiding mistakes and presenting a polished program, we will develop the program in a logical manner, commit the mistakes, recognize that mistakes have been made, and rewrite the program until it correctly performs the task. We proceed in this way because it more accurately reflects how complicated programs are written. We should be aware that throughout the development of a complex program, we are increasing our knowledge of the task. During this time we should constantly be on guard for errors in the program or for discrepancies between the program and the specification of the task.

Figure 5–14 illustrates one possible initial situation for this task. We use this situation to create a general plan for escaping from rooms. Initially, Karel is somewhere in the room, facing some arbitrary direction. The robot starts the task by moving to the wall that it is initially facing. Karel then follows the inside perimeter of the room in a counterclockwise direction, keeping its right side to the wall, until it senses the door on its right. Karel next exits through the door and finally turns itself off. Translating this informally stated escape plan, we obtain the following program.

```
BEGINNING-OF-EXECUTION
  go-to-wall;
  turnleft;
  follow-until-door-is-on-right;
  exit-door;
  turnoff
END-OF-EXECUTION
```

This program accomplishes the task, but in order to have Karel understand it, we must first define the instructions `go-to-wall`, `follow-until-door-is-on-right`, and `exit-door`. We begin by writing the `go-to-wall` instruction. This instruction must move Karel forward until the robot senses a wall directly in front blocking its path. The test we eventually want to become true is `front-is-blocked`, so we should be able to write this instruction as follows.

```
DEFINE-NEW-INSTRUCTION go-to-wall AS
  BEGIN
    WHILE front-is-clear DO
      move
  END;
```

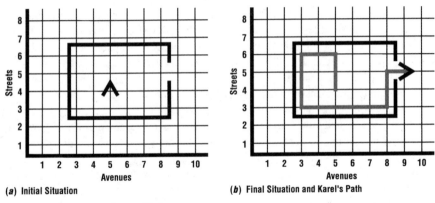

(*a*) Initial Situation

(*b*) Final Situation and Karel's Path

Figure 5–14   A Room-Escape Task

Although this simple instruction works in Figure 5–14 and in many other similar initial situations, it does not work correctly in all initial situations. Unfortunately, in some initial situations the **WHILE** instruction never terminates, leaving Karel in an infinite loop. The common element in these situations is that Karel starts the task already facing toward the door, instead of toward one of the walls. When Karel executes the **go-to-wall** instruction in such a situation, the robot zooms out of the room without knowing that it has exited. One situation of this type is illustrated in Figure 5–15.

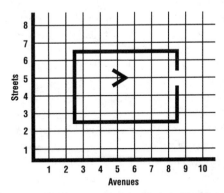

Figure 5–15   A Beyond-the-Horizon Situation for the Room-Escape Task

We call this type of situation a beyond-the-horizon situation. Normally, we write a program guided by a few initial situations that seem to cover all interesting aspects of the task. Although we would like to prove that all other situations are not too different from these sample situations, frequently the best we can do is hope. As we explore the problem and learn more about the task, we may discover situations that are beyond our original horizons—situations that are legal but special trouble-causing cases. Once we have discovered a beyond-the-horizon situation, we should immediately simulate Karel's execution in it. If our suspicions are confirmed, and Karel does not perform as we intended, we must modify our program accordingly.

Let's construct a simple numerical argument that calculates the probability of finding a beyond-the-horizon situation by randomly testing Karel in legal initial situations. We restrict the following discussion to the room pictured in Figure 5–15. If we included all possible room sizes and door locations, the problems we would encounter would become more severe.

In our example room, there are 24 possible corners on which Karel can start this task. Moreover, there are four ways that Karel can be placed on each corner (the four directions that can be faced). Consequently, there are 96 different initial situations in which Karel can start this task. Out of this possible 96, only 6 placements of Karel can cause trouble for the go-to-wall instruction—Karel facing east on any of the six corners on 5th Street. Thus, Karel malfunctions in less than 7 percent of all its possible starting positions. This argument demonstrates that randomly testing Karel in different initial situations is most likely to be ineffective. We must use our intellect to try to uncover those few situations where Karel's program may malfunction.

We must think hard to discover these situations, because they are not in our intuitive field of view. However, our time is profitably spent doing so, because looking for beyond-the-horizon situations can only benefit us: if we find situations that cause errors, we can correct our program to account for them; if we cannot find any situations that cause errors, we have made progress toward convincing ourselves that our program is correct. Good programmers become skilled at extending their horizons and finding dangerous situations that prevent a program from accomplishing its task.

Returning to Karel's task, what can we do to correct our program? The basic plan is still valid, but we must modify the go-to-wall instruction, making sure that Karel finds the wall before it accidentally exits the room. The fact that the door is only one block wide is the key to our next attempt at writing go-to-wall. Instead of moving Karel straight ahead, we will program Karel to move forward in a sideways shuffling motion.

Karel starts by checking for a wall directly in front of itself; if the robot does not find one, it next checks for a wall in front of the corner on its right. If Karel does not find walls in either of these places, it returns to its original corner and then moves one block forward. Karel repeats this right–left shuffling motion until it finds a wall. In this way Karel is guaranteed not to pass through the unnoticed door, because the door is only one block wide. The path Karel takes in the beyond-the-horizon situation is displayed in Figure 5–16. This same type of path works correctly in Figure 5–14, too.

So now let's rewrite go-to-wall to correspond to our new plan for moving Karel to a wall. We again use a WHILE loop with the same test, but in this instruction Karel's forward motion is more complicated.

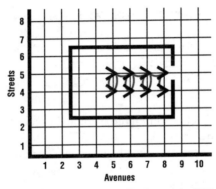

Figure 5–16   Karel's Shuffle Toward the Wall

```
DEFINE-NEW-INSTRUCTION go-to-wall AS
BEGIN
    WHILE front-is-clear DO
    shuffle
END;
```

We continue by using stepwise refinement to write `shuffle`.

```
DEFINE-NEW-INSTRUCTION shuffle AS
BEGIN
    sidestep-right;
    IF front-is-clear THEN
        BEGIN
            sidestep-back-left;
            move
        END
END;
```

Finally, we write the simple sidestepping instructions directly in terms of `move`, `turnleft`, and `turnright`.

```
DEFINE-NEW-INSTRUCTION sidestep-right AS
BEGIN
    turnright;
    move;
    turnleft
END;
```

and

```
DEFINE-NEW-INSTRUCTION sidestep-back-left AS
  BEGIN
    turnleft;
    move;
    turnright
  END;
```

Simulate these instructions in Figure 5–14 and Figure 5–15 to become better acquainted with this `go-to-wall` instruction.

Even this plan, however, has a small hidden wart on it; in some initial situations Karel cannot perform a shuffle. For example, look at the new beyond-the-horizon situation illustrated in Figure 5–17.

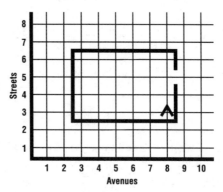

Figure 5–17 A Beyond-the-Horizon Situation That Prevents Shuffling

The wall on Karel's right prevents it from correctly performing the shuffle. Luckily, in situations like Figure 5–17, all we must do is turn Karel to the right; it will then be facing a wall, which easily satisfies the intent of `go-to-wall`. So, if Karel starts this task with its right side blocked by a wall, the robot merely turns to face this wall. Otherwise, its right is not blocked by a wall, and it can shuffle forward and to the right until its front becomes blocked. To accomplish this modification, we must rewrite only the definition of `go-to-wall`.

```
DEFINE-NEW-INSTRUCTION go-to-wall AS
  BEGIN
    IF right-is-blocked THEN
      turnright
    ELSE
      WHILE front-is-clear DO
        shuffle
  END;
```

Well, as you may have suspected, there still is a problem with `go-to-wall`. This problem is illustrated in Figure 5–18, one of the most blatant beyond-the-horizon situations we may ever see; it is the single situation in which the present

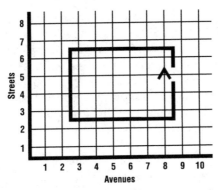

Figure 5–18 A Beyond-the-Horizon Situation
That Causes an Error Shutoff

go-to-wall instruction fails. This is the last difficulty we will see before completing a correct version of go-to-wall, so please don't get disgusted and stop reading.

If Karel executes our current go-to-wall instruction in this initial situation, the robot will think that it can shuffle to the wall ahead—because its right is clear. So Karel starts executing the WHILE loop in the ELSE clause of go-to-wall. Karel first finds that its front is clear, which means that the robot will execute the shuffle. The shuffle instruction moves Karel out of the door, where its front is still clear, then Karel moves back inside of the room and one block forward. This instruction leaves the robot facing north on 6th Street and 8th Avenue. Although Karel's actions look strange, nothing is terribly wrong; after all, Karel is still looking in front of itself for a wall. Karel next rechecks front-is-clear in the WHILE loop and finds it true again, so Karel again starts to execute shuffle. This time, however, the robot is stopped by an error shutoff in sidestep-right, which commands it to turn right and then move—an impossibility in its current situation.

The problem is that we thought that Karel's right side could never become blocked if it was not originally blocked in its initial situation. Figure 5–18 showed us that this assumption is incorrect. We must modify go-to-wall so that Karel always checks to its right before executing a shuffle. This modification has been done in the following, finally correct definition of go-to-wall. Notice that the final definition consists of a WHILE loop that tests front-is-clear, so when this instruction finishes executing—and now we know that it always will—Karel's front is guaranteed to be blocked by one of the walls in the room.

```
DEFINE-NEW-INSTRUCTION go-to-wall AS
  BEGIN
    WHILE front-is-clear DO
      IF right-is-blocked THEN
        turnright
      ELSE shuffle
  END;
```

The `go-to-wall` instruction now works correctly in any room. After executing `go-to-wall`, Karel will always have its front blocked by one of the four walls in the room. Because this instruction is so complicated and crucial to the task, we should immediately simulate Karel's execution of it in the initial situations illustrated in Figures 5–15 through 5–19. We should not proceed until we are familiar with exactly how Karel executes each instruction and we know what part each instruction plays in moving Karel to a wall.

Next we will write the `follow-until-door-is-on-right` instruction. Recall that in the initial plan, Karel executes a `turnleft` instruction after `go-to-wall`; therefore, we can safely assume that just before Karel executes `follow-until-door-is-on-right`, its right is blocked by one wall of the room. This new instruction must satisfy two criteria.

- It must finish when Karel senses a door on its right-hand side. Karel senses this door when its right becomes clear.

- If a door has not been found, the instruction must keep Karel's right side adjacent to a wall while commanding it to follow the perimeter of the room in a counterclockwise direction.

We can extend the notion of an invariant to apply for the duration of an entire instruction (instead of just a loop). The invariant for the second criterion above is that Karel's right-hand side must be adjacent to a wall (blocked) as it follows the perimeter of the room. To do this, Karel moves forward along a wall until it reaches a corner; when this happens, it turns left, ready to follow the next wall with its right side still blocked.

We begin by using the first criterion to write the instruction that finds the door. Karel must maneuver itself into a situation in which its right side is clear, so we again use a **WHILE** instruction to write our definition.

```
DEFINE-NEW-INSTRUCTION follow-until-door-is-on-right AS
    BEGIN
        WHILE right-is-blocked DO
            follow-perimeter
    END;
```

Provided that this loop terminates, Karel's right-hand side will be clear when the robot finishes executing `follow-until-door-is-on-right`. We now use the second criterion to write the `follow-perimeter` instruction.

```
    DEFINE-NEW-INSTRUCTION follow-perimeter AS
        BEGIN
            IF front-is-clear THEN
                move
            ELSE turnleft
        END;
```

This instruction moves Karel forward along a wall until it reaches a corner. Whenever it reaches a corner, Karel performs a left turn and is ready to continue following the perimeter with its right-hand side next to the new wall. The invariant that its right side is always next to a wall remains true until it finally senses that the door is on its right-hand side.

Finally, we write the **exit-door** instruction. This is easy to do because it contains no complicated subparts. We can safely assume that Karel's right side is clear, since this instruction is executed directly after **follow-until-door-is-on-right**. The **exit-door** instruction can be written by using only Karel's primitive instructions and **turnright**.

```
DEFINE-NEW-INSTRUCTION exit-door AS
   BEGIN
      turnright;
      move
   END;
```

We have now specified every instruction that Karel needs to accomplish its task. Although we cannot verify correctness, we should at least be able to verify that execution errors cannot occur. We can do this by showing that Karel never tries to execute a **move** instruction—the only primitive instruction in this program capable of causing an error shutoff—when its front is blocked. We hope that this section has demonstrated how a difficult task can be programmed successfully by using the stepwise refinement programming method. The entire program for this task is as follows.

```
BEGINNING-OF-PROGRAM

DEFINE-NEW-INSTRUCTION turnright AS
 BEGIN
  ITERATE 3 TIMES
    turnleft
 END;

DEFINE-NEW-INSTRUCTION sidestep-right AS
 BEGIN
  turnright;
  move;
  turnleft
 END;

DEFINE-NEW-INSTRUCTION sidestep-back-left AS
 BEGIN
  turnleft;
  move;
  turnright
 END;
```

```
DEFINE-NEW-INSTRUCTION shuffle AS
 BEGIN
  sidestep-right;
  IF front-is-clear THEN
    BEGIN
      sidestep-back-left;
      move
    END
 END;

DEFINE-NEW-INSTRUCTION go-to-wall AS
 BEGIN
   WHILE front-is-clear DO
     IF right-is-blocked THEN
       turnright
     ELSE shuffle
 END;

DEFINE-NEW-INSTRUCTION follow-perimeter AS
 BEGIN
   IF front-is-clear THEN
     move
   ELSE turnleft
 END;

DEFINE-NEW-INSTRUCTION follow-until-door-is-on-right AS
 BEGIN
   WHILE right-is-blocked DO
     follow-perimeter
 END;

DEFINE-NEW-INSTRUCTION exit-door AS
 BEGIN
   turnright;
   move
 END;

BEGINNING-OF-EXECUTION
   go-to-wall;
   turnleft;
   follow-until-door-is-on-right;
   exit-door;
   turnoff
END-OF-EXECUTION

END-OF-PROGRAM
```

Before leaving this example, what would Karel do in the beyond-the-horizon situations illustrated in Figure 5–19? In both situations, Karel successfully escapes from the room and turns itself off, but not quite in the manner we might expect. Which instruction(s) must we change to remove the slight flaw from Karel's performance in the "unexpected door" situation on the right? In this initial situation, Karel should exit the room and then turn itself off when it reaches the corner of 8th Street and 6th Avenue.

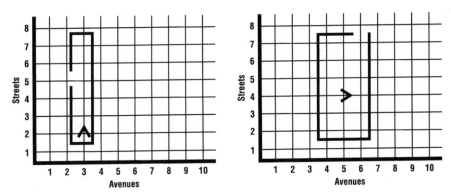

Figure 5–19   Two Beyond-the-Horizon Situations

Although we believe that this program is correct, there still may be other, undiscovered, beyond-the-horizon situations that force it to fail. Our minds are still open on the subject. This attitude is not false modesty; in earlier versions of this book, we incorrectly wrote the `go-to-wall` instruction by not discovering the beyond-the-horizon situation illustrated in Figure 5–19. Writing a completely, no-doubts-about-it, 100 percent correct program, even for a seemingly simple task like this one, is a very difficult endeavor.

When attempting to write a large program, we must not succumb to the "We've got to get it perfect the first time" syndrome. This kind of thinking leads to programmer's block: the inability to begin writing a program. The most important step toward writing a program is putting something concrete down on paper. Once this is done, we can test the program by simulation, spot errors, and revise the program to remedy the errors. With nothing written down, however, progress will be slow—and frustration will be high. Remember that a correct program is only half a solution, and we must make sure that our program is also easy to understand and easy to modify.

Finally, if we revise the program to the point that we lose the original thread of reasoning, we may have to rewrite the entire program. Rewriting a program is not as time consuming as it may seem because we can use all the knowledge that we gained while writing the previous versions. Remember that no program is a complete disaster; it can always be used as a bad example.

5.8 WHEN TO USE A REPEATING INSTRUCTION

As explained at the end of the last chapter, a decision map is a technique that asks questions about the problem we are trying to solve. The answers to the questions determine which path of the map to follow. If we have done a thorough job of planning our implementation, the decision map should suggest an appropriate instruction to use. Examine some of the discussions presented in this chapter and see how the complete decision map that is presented in Figure 5–20 might have been useful.

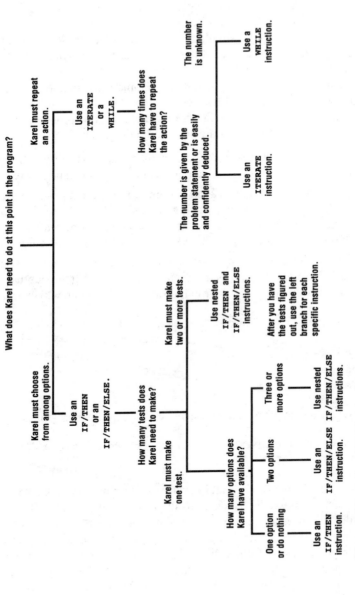

Figure 5–20 A Complete Decision Map

5.9 PROBLEM SET

The problems in this section require writing definitions and programs that use ITERATE and WHILE instructions. Try using stepwise refinement and the four-step process discussed in Section 5.2.3 when writing these definitions and programs. Test your solutions by simulating them in various initial situations, and try to find beyond-the-horizon situations too. Take care to write programs that avoid error shutoffs and infinite loops.

A common mistake among beginning programmers is trying to have each execution of a WHILE loop's body make too much progress. As a rule of thumb, try to have each execution of a WHILE loop's body make as little progress as possible (while still making some progress toward terminating the loop).

1. Write a new instruction for Karel named **empty-beeper-bag**. After Karel executes this instruction, its beeper-bag should be empty.

2. Write a new instruction called **go-to-origin** that positions Karel on 1st Street and 1st Avenue facing east, regardless of its initial location or the direction it is initially facing. Assume that no wall sections are present. *Hint:* Use the south and west boundary walls as guides.

3. Study both of the following program fragments separately. What does each do? For each one, is there a simpler program fragment that is execution equivalent? If so, write it down; if not, explain why not.

```
WHILE not-next-to-a-beeper DO    WHILE not-next-to-a-beeper DO
    move;                            IF next-to-a-beeper THEN
If next-to-a-beeper THEN                 pickbeeper
    pickbeeper                       ELSE move
ELSE move
```

Describe the difference between the following two program fragments:

```
WHILE front-is-clear DO      IF front-is-clear THEN
    move                         move
```

4. There is a menace in Karel's world—an infinite pile of beepers. Yes, it sounds impossible, but occasionally it occurs in the world. If Karel accidentally tries to pick up an infinite pile of beepers, it is forever doomed to pick beepers from the pile. Karel's current situation places the robot in grave danger from such a pile. The robot is standing outside of two rooms: one is to the west and one is to the east. Only one of these rooms has a pile of beepers that Karel can pick. The other room has the dreaded infinite pile of beepers. Karel must decide which room is the safe room, enter it, and pick all of the beepers. To help the robot decide which room is safe, there is a third pile of beepers on the corner at which Karel is currently standing. If this third pile has an even number of beepers, the

safe room is the eastern room. If the pile has an odd number of beepers, the safe room is the western room. There is at least one beeper in the third pile. Program Karel to pick the beepers in the safe room (Figure 5–21).

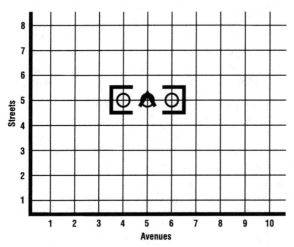

Figure 5–21   A Very Dangerous Task

5. Karel must place beepers in the exact arrangement shown in Figure 5–22. Karel has exactly enough beepers for the task and always starts on the bottom-left corner of the square.

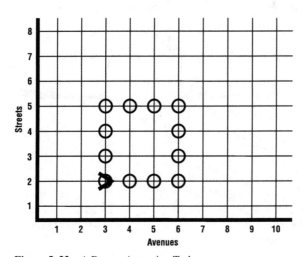

Figure 5–22   A Beeper Arranging Task

6. Program Karel to escape from a rectangular room if it can find a doorway. If there is no doorway, the robot must turn itself off. We cannot use the program written in Section 5.7 for this task, because executing this program in a doorless room would cause Karel to run around inside the room forever; can you identify the instruction that will never finish executing? *Hint:* There is a slightly messy way to solve this problem without resorting to beepers. You can write the program this way, or you can assume that Karel has one beeper in the beeper-bag, which it can use to remember if it has circumnavigated the room. This program may require a separate **turnoff** instruction for the completely enclosed situation in addition to a **turnoff** instruction for the situation with a door.

7. Karel is working once again as a gardener. The robot must outline the wall segment shown in Figure 5–23 with beepers. One and only one beeper is to be planted on each corner that is adjacent to a wall. You may assume that Karel always starts in the same relative position and has exactly enough beepers to do the task.

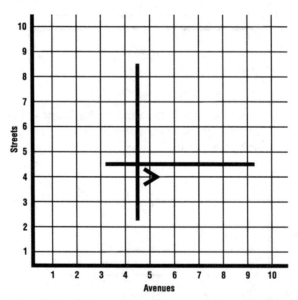

Figure 5–23 Another Gardening Job

8. Karel's beeper crop failed again. The robot is back to carpeting hallways. The hallways always have the same general shape as shown in Figure 5–24 and are always one block wide. To ensure there are no lumps in the carpet, only one beeper can be placed on a corner. Karel has exactly enough beepers to do the job and always starts in the same relative location.

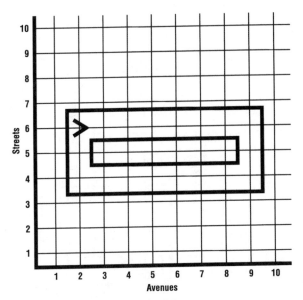

Figure 5–24 Another Carpeting Job

9. Program Karel to run a super steeplechase. In this race the hurdles are arbitrarily high, and the course has no fixed finish corner. The finish of each race course is marked by a beeper, which Karel must pick up before turning itself off. Figure 5–25 illustrates one possible course. Other courses may be longer and have higher hurdles.

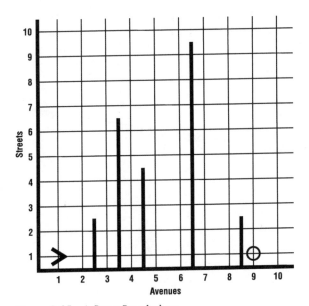

Figure 5–25 A Super Steeplechase

10. Program Karel to run a super-duper steeplechase. In this race the hurdles are arbitrarily high and arbitrarily wide. In each race course the finish is marked by a beeper, which Karel must pick up before turning itself off. Figure 5–26 illustrates one possible race course.

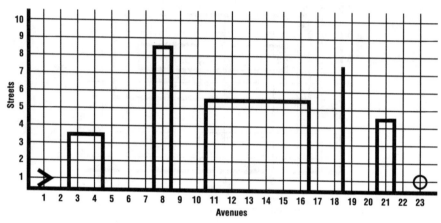

Figure 5–26   A Super-Duper Steeplechase

11. Write an instruction that harvests a rectangular field of any size. The field is guaranteed to be bordered by beeperless corners. In addition, assume that every corner within the field has a beeper on it and that Karel starts out facing east on the lower left-hand corner of the field.

12. Karel has returned to the diamond-shaped beeper field to harvest a new crop (Figure 5–27). Write a new program for Karel that harvests the beepers. The beeper field is always the same size, and there is always one beeper on each corner of the field.

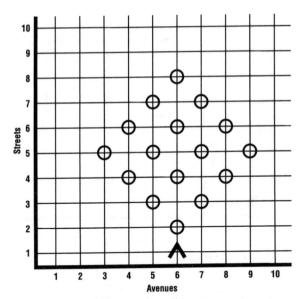

Streets

Avenues

Figure 5–27   Return to the Diamond-Shaped Beeper Field

13.   Karel is building a fence. The fence will be made of beepers and will surround a rectangular-shaped wall segment. The size of the wall segment is unknown. Karel is at the origin facing an unknown direction. The fences (beepers) are stacked somewhere next to the western boundary wall. There are exactly enough beepers in the pile to build the fence. The beeper pile is on the street that is adjacent to the southern edge of the wall segment as shown in Figure 5–28. The distances to the beeper pile and to the wall segment are unknown. Program Karel to build the fence and return to the origin. Assume that there are no beepers in Karel's beeper-bag at the start of the program.

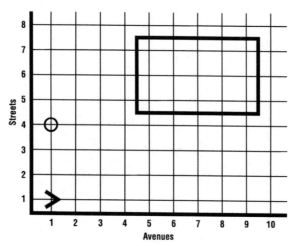

Figure 5–28   Building a Fence

14. Karel likes to take long meandering walks in the woods in the world, and even though it has a built-in compass, the robot sometimes cannot find its way back home. To alleviate this problem, before Karel walks in the woods the robot fills its beeper-bag and then it leaves a trail of beepers. Program Karel to follow this path back home. We can ask many questions about this task. Ignore the possibility that any wall boundaries or wall sections interfere with Karel, and assume that the end of the path is marked by two beepers on the same corner. Each beeper will be reachable from the previous beeper by the execution of one move. In addition, the path will never cross over itself. See Figure 5–29 for a path that Karel must follow. *Hint:* Karel must probe each possible next corner in the path, eventually finding the correct one. It might prove useful to have Karel pick up the beepers as it follows the path; otherwise it may get caught in an infinite loop going backward and forward. How difficult would it be to program Karel to follow the same type of path if we allowed for a beeper to be missing once in a while (but not two missing beepers in a row)?

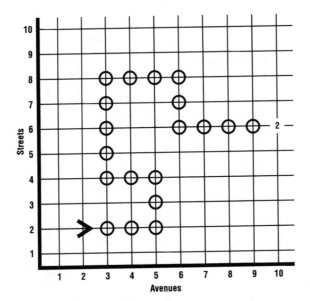

Figure 5–29 A Path of Beepers

15. Assume that Karel is somewhere in a completely enclosed rectangular room that contains one beeper. Program Karel to find the beeper, pick it up, and turn itself off.

16. Program Karel to escape from a maze that contains no islands. The exit of the maze is marked by placing a beeper on the first corner that is outside the maze, next to the right wall. This task can be accomplished by commanding Karel to move through the maze, with the invariant that its right side is always next to a wall. See Problem 4.10–9 for hints on the type of movements for which Karel must be programmed. Figure 5–30 shows one example of a maze.

There is a simpler way to program this task without using the instructions written in Problem 4.10–9. Try to write a shorter version of the maze-escaping program. *Hint:* Program Karel to make the minimal amount of progress toward its goal at each corner in the maze.

Finally, compare the maze-escape problem with Problem 5.9–10, the super-duper steeplechase. Do you see any similarities?

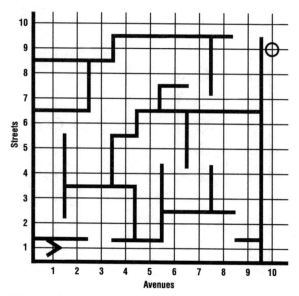

Figure 5–30 A Maze

17. This problem is inspired by the discussion on the verification of **WHILE** loops (Section 5.6). Simulate Karel's execution of the following instruction in initial situations where the robot is on a corner with 0, 1, 2, 3, and 7 beepers.

```
DEFINE-NEW-INSTRUCTION will-this-clear-corner-of-beepers AS
BEGIN
    ITERATE 10 TIMES
        IF next-to-a-beeper THEN
        pickbeeper
END;
```

State in exactly which initial situations this instruction works correctly. What happens in the other situations?

18. Program Karel to go on a treasure hunt. The treasure is marked by a corner containing five beepers. Other corners (including the corner on which Karel starts) contain clues, with each clue indicating in which direction Karel should proceed. The clues are as follows: 1 beeper means Karel should go north, 2 means west, 3 means south, and 4 means east. Karel should follow the clues until it reaches the treasure corner where the robot should turn itself off. Figure 5–31 shows one possible treasure hunt.

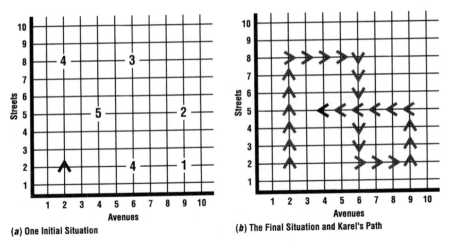

(*a*) One Initial Situation

(*b*) The Final Situation and Karel's Path

Figure 5–31   A Treasure Hunt

19.   Karel is inside a room that has a number of open windows. There are no windows in the corners of the room. Karel is next to the northern wall facing east. Program Karel to close the windows by putting one beeper in front of each window (Figure 5–32). You may assume that Karel has exactly enough beepers to complete the task.

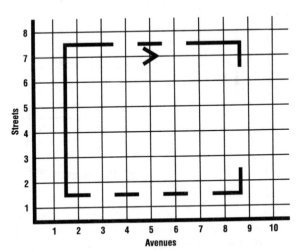

Figure 5–32   Closing the Windows

20. Karel is at the origin facing east. In front of Karel, somewhere along 1st Street, is a line of beepers. (One beeper is on each corner, with at least one beeper in the line.) The length of the line of beepers is unknown, but there are no gaps in the line. Karel must pick up and move the beepers north a number of streets equal to the number of beepers in the line. For example, if there are five beepers in the line, the beepers must be moved to 6th Street. The beepers must be moved directly north. If the first beeper is on 4th Avenue, it must be on 4th Avenue when the program is finished.

21. Karel is inside a completely enclosed room with no doors or windows. The robot is in the southeast corner facing south. There is one wall segment inside the room with Karel. The wall segment blocks north/south travel and does not touch the walls that form the room. On one side of the wall segment is a beeper (which side is unknown). Program Karel to find and move the beeper to the opposite side of the wall segment (Figure 5–33).

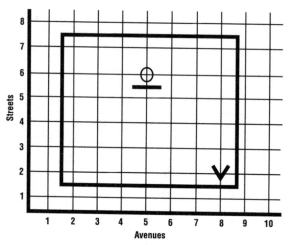

Figure 5–33 Finding and Moving a Beeper

22. Once again Karel is working as a carpet layer. Before carpeting a room, Karel must ensure that the room has continuous walls to the west, north, and east. Only these rooms must be carpeted. The doors to the rooms are always to the south. All rooms are one block wide, and there is always a northern wall at the end of each room. Karel's task ends when the robot arrives at a blocking wall segment on 1st Street. Figure 5–34 shows one possible set of initial and final situations.

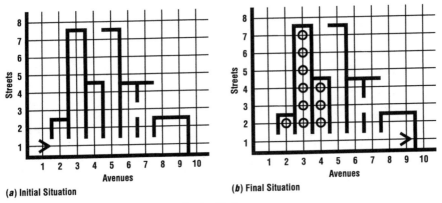

(a) Initial Situation   (b) Final Situation

Figure 5-34   A More Complex Carpet Laying Task

23.   Program Karel to arrange vertical piles of beepers into ascending order. Each avenue, starting at the origin, will contain a vertical pile of one or more beepers. The first empty avenue will mark the end of the piles that need to be sorted. Figure 5-35 illustrates one of the many possible initial and final situations. (How difficult would it be to modify your program to arrange the piles of beepers into descending order?)

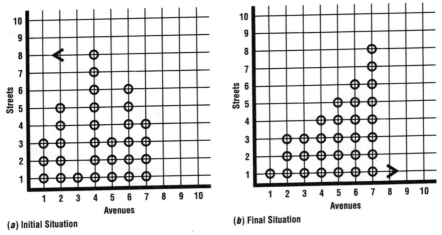

(a) Initial Situation   (b) Final Situation

Figure 5-35   A Sorting Task

6 ADVANCED TECHNIQUES FOR KAREL

This chapter presents three quite challenging topics. The first is a new control structure for Karel called recursion. Recursion, like loops, allows Karel to execute a sequence of statements more than once. The other sections concern two interesting new instructions that provide Karel with the ability to solve some novel beeper-manipulation problems, including numerical computations. All are advanced topics and are presented in this chapter because they may not be covered in all courses. (Or, in the case of recursion, they may not be allowed by your software simulator.)

6.1 RECURSION

Having thoroughly looked at loops in the last chapter, we are now going to examine another method of making Karel repetitively execute a sequence of instructions. When a programming language allows recursive definitions or recursion, it means that a new instruction can call itself (use its own name) within its own definition. This may seem odd at first, but after a few examples, we hope that it will appear as natural as using a **WHILE** loop to control Karel's execution. We note that recursion is just another control structure and, while it may appear magical at first, it can be understood as readily as loops. It is another programming tool to add to your collection.

Given the problem—Karel must face north starting from an initially unknown direction—we would probably write a loop that looks like the following.

```
DEFINE-NEW-INSTRUCTION face-north AS
    BEGIN
        WHILE not-facing-north DO
            BEGIN
                turnleft
            END
    END;
```

This correctly solves the problem and is known as an iterative solution. ("Iterative" does not imply that an `ITERATE` instruction was used, but rather that a loop of some sort, `WHILE` or `ITERATE`, was used.) Contrast this solution with a recursive one.

```
DEFINE-NEW-INSTRUCTION face-north AS
   BEGIN
      IF not-facing-north  THEN
         BEGIN
            turnleft;
            face-north
         END
   END;
```

The difference between these two instructions is very subtle. The first instruction, which uses the `WHILE` loop, is called once, and Karel's focus never leaves the instruction until it is finished with the loop, executing anywhere from 0 to 3 `turnlefts` (depending on the initial direction the robot is facing). What happens in the second, recursive, `face-north`? Let's look at it very carefully.

If Karel is initially facing north when the instruction is called, nothing happens (similar to the `WHILE` loop). If Karel is facing east when the instruction is called, the `IF` test is true, so Karel executes one `turnleft` instruction (thus facing north) and then makes a second call of `face-north`, remembering where it was in the first call. When `face-north` is called the second time, the `IF` test is false, so nothing happens and Karel returns to the first call.

```
[initial instantiation of]
DEFINE-NEW-INSTRUCTION face-north AS
   BEGIN
      IF not-facing-north  THEN
         BEGIN
            turnleft;
            face-north        [→ This is the second call to
         END                   face-north. Karel will return
   END;                        to this point when that call
                               finishes executing.]

[second instantiation of]
DEFINE-NEW-INSTRUCTION face-north AS
   BEGIN
      IF not-facing-north  THEN   [→ this is now false]
         BEGIN
            turnleft;
            face-north
         END
   END;
```

Each call results in a separate instance (or instantiation) of the instruction `face-north`. Karel must completely execute each instance, always remembering where it was in the previous instance so it can return there when it finishes.

The process for writing recursive Karel instructions is very similar to that for writing loops:

Step 1: Consider the stopping condition (also called the base case). What is the simplest case of the problem that can be solved? In the `face-north` problem, the simplest, or base, case is when Karel is already facing north.

Step 2: What does Karel have to do in the base case? In this case there's nothing to do.

Step 3: Find a way to solve a small piece of the larger problem if not in the base case. This is called "reducing the problem in the general case." In the `face-north` problem, the general case is when Karel is not facing north and the reduction is to turn left.

Step 4: Make sure the reduction leads to the base case. Again, in the above example of `face-north`, by turning left one 90-degree increment at a time, Karel must eventually face north, regardless of its initial direction.

Let's compare and contrast iteration and recursion:

- An iterative loop must complete each iteration before beginning the next one.

- A recursive instruction typically begins a new instance before completing the current one. When that happens, the current instance is temporarily suspended, pending the completion of the new instance. Of course, this new instance might not complete before generating another one. Each successive instance must be completed in turn, last to first.

- Since each recursive instance is supposed to make minimal progress toward the base case, we should not use loops to control recursive calls. Thus, we will usually see an **IF/THEN** or an **IF/THEN/ELSE** in the body of a recursive new instruction.

Suppose we wanted to use recursion to move Karel to a beeper. How would we do it? Following the steps presented earlier:

- What is the base case? Karel is on the beeper.
- What does Karel have to do in the base case? Nothing.
- What is the general case? Karel is not on the beeper.
- What is the reduction? Move toward the beeper and make the recursive call.
- Does the reduction lead to termination? Yes, assuming the beeper is directly in front of Karel, the distance will get shorter by one block for each recursive call.

The final implementation follows.

```
DEFINE-NEW-INSTRUCTION find-beeper AS
  BEGIN
    IF not-next-to-a-beeper   THEN
      BEGIN
        move;
        find-beeper
      END
  END;
```

Note that this problem could also have been easily solved with a **WHILE** loop. Let's look at a problem that is not easily solved with a **WHILE** loop. Remember the *Lost Beeper Mine,* the corner with a large number of beepers? Imagine we must write the following instruction in our search for the mine. Karel must walk east from its current location until it finds a beeper. The *Lost Beeper Mine* is due north of that intersection a distance equal to the number of moves Karel made to get from its current position to the beeper. Write the new instruction, **find-mine.**

It is not easy to see how to solve this problem with a **WHILE** loop, for we do not have any convenient way of remembering how many intersections have been traversed. Oh, we could probably come up with a very convoluted beeper-tracking scheme, but let's take a look at a recursive solution that's pretty straightforward. Again, we'll answer our questions:

- What is the base case? Karel is on the beeper.
- What does Karel have to do in the base case? **turnleft.** (This will face Karel north.)
- What is the general case? Karel is not on the beeper.
- What is the reduction? Move one block forward, make the recursive call, and have Karel execute a second **move** after the recursive call. This second **move** will be executed in all instances but the base case, causing Karel to make as many moves north after the base case as it did in getting to the base case.
- Does the reduction lead to termination? Yes, assuming the beeper is directly in front of Karel.

Let's look at the complete instruction:

```
DEFINE-NEW-INSTRUCTION find-mine AS
  BEGIN
    IF next-to-a-beeper   THEN
      BEGIN
        turnleft
      END
    ELSE
      BEGIN
        move;
        find-mine;
        move
      END
  END;
```

How many **turnlefts** are executed? How many **moves**? How many calls to **find-mine**?

A number of problems will have to be solved and a good deal of thinking will have to take place before recursion becomes as comfortable to use as iteration. This will be necessary largely because recursion requires some intuition to see the correct reduction, especially in difficult problems. This intuition will come with practice, which is precisely what the sample problems are designed to provide.

6.2 SEARCHING

This section introduces two defined instructions named **zig-left-up** and **zag-down-right**, which move Karel diagonally northwest and southeast respectively. Both instructions are defined by using only Karel's primitive instructions and **turnright**, but we derive immense conceptual power from being able to think in terms of Karel moving diagonally.

The following definitions introduce the stars of this section: **zig-left-up** and **zag-down-right**. These direction pairs are not arbitrary; if Karel moves to the left and upward long enough, it eventually reaches the western boundary wall. The same argument holds for traveling down and toward the right, except that in this case Karel eventually reaches the southern boundary wall.

The other two possible direction pairs lack these useful properties: Karel will never find a boundary wall by traveling up and toward the right, and we cannot be sure which of the two boundary walls it will come upon first when traveling downward and to the left.

The following instructions define **zig-left-up** and **zag-down-right**.

```
DEFINE-NEW-INSTRUCTION zig-left-up AS
  BEGIN
    move;
    turnright;
    move;
    turnleft
  END;

DEFINE-NEW-INSTRUCTION zag-down-right AS
  BEGIN
    move;
    turnleft;
    move;
    turnright
  END;
```

Observe that no part of these instructions forces Karel to move in the intended directions. To execute **zig-left-up** correctly, Karel must be facing west; to execute **zag-down-right** correctly, Karel must be facing south. These requirements are called the <u>preconditions</u> of the instructions—that is, conditions that must be made true before Karel can correctly execute the instruction. We have seen other examples of preconditions in this book, although we did not give them a special name until now.

For this example, the directional precondition of `zig-left-up` is that Karel is facing west; similarly, the directional precondition of `zag-down-right` is that Karel is facing south. Karel's execution of these instructions, when their preconditions are satisfied, is shown in Figure 6–1.

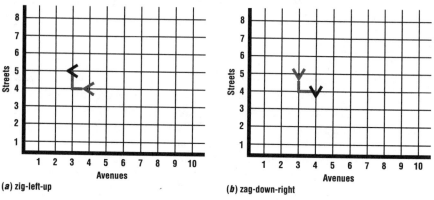

(**a**) zig-left-up   (**b**) zag-down-right

Figure 6–1   Execution of the Zig-Zag Instruction

Here is a statement that is loaded with terminology: the directional preconditions of `zig-left-up` and `zag-down-right` are invariant over each instruction's execution. This simply means that if Karel is facing west and it executes `zig-left-up`, the robot is still facing west after the instruction has finished executing. This property allows Karel to execute a sequence of `zig-left-up`'s without having to reestablish their directional precondition. A similar statement holds about Karel's facing south and `zag-down-right`. Also observe that each instruction must be executed only when Karel's front is clear. This precondition is not invariant over the instructions, because Karel may be one block away from a corner where its front is blocked (e.g., Karel may execute `zig-left-up` while facing west on the corner of 4th Street and 2nd Avenue).

The first major instruction that we will write solves the problem of finding a beeper that can be located anywhere in the world. Our task is to write an instruction named `find-beeper` that positions Karel on the same corner as the beeper. We have seen a version of this problem in Chapter 5 where both Karel and the beeper are in an enclosed room. This new formulation has less stringent restrictions: the beeper is placed on some arbitrary street corner in Karel's world, and there are no wall sections in the world. Of course, the boundary walls are always present.

One simple solution may spring to mind. In this attempt, Karel first goes to the origin and faces east. The robot then moves eastward on 1st Street looking for a beeper. If Karel finds a beeper on 1st Street, it has accomplished its task; if the beeper is not found on 1st Street, Karel moves back to the western wall, switches over to 2nd Street, and continues searching from there. Karel repeats this strategy until it finds the beeper. Unfortunately, there is a mistaken assumption implicit in this search method: Karel has no way of knowing that the beeper is not on 1st Street. No matter how much of 1st Street Karel explores, the robot can never be sure that the beeper is not one block farther east.

It appears that we and Karel are caught in an impossible trap, but there is an ingenious solution to our problem. As we might expect, it involves zig-zag moves. We need to program Karel to perform a radically different type of search pattern. Figure 6–2 shows such a pattern, and we use it below to define the **find-beeper** instruction.

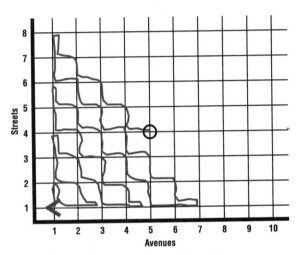

Figure 6–2   A Method for Searching Every Corner

This search method expands the search frontier much as water would expand over Karel's world from an overflowing sink at the origin. Roughly, we can view Karel as traveling back and forth diagonally on the fringe of this water wave. Convince yourself that this search pattern is guaranteed to find the beeper eventually, regardless of the beeper's location. In our analogy, we need to convince ourselves that the beeper will eventually get wet. We can use stepwise refinement to write the **find-beeper** instruction, using this search method with the **zig-left-up** and **zag-down-right** instructions.

```
DEFINE-NEW-INSTRUCTION find-beeper AS
  BEGIN
    go-to-origin;
    face-west;
    WHILE not-next-to-a-beeper DO
      IF facing-west THEN
        zig-move
      ELSE
        zag-move
  END;
```

The **find-beeper** instruction starts by moving Karel to the origin and then facing west. These instructions establish the directional precondition for **zig-left-up**. The WHILE loop's purpose is to keep Karel moving until it finds a beeper, and the loop is correct if it eventually terminates. The IF condition, which is nested within the body of the loop, determines the direction in which Karel has been traveling and continues moving the robot along the diagonal in this same direction. We continue the stepwise refinement by writing **zig-move** and **zag-move**.

```
DEFINE-NEW-INSTRUCTION zig-move AS
  BEGIN
    IF front-is-clear THEN
      zig-left-up
    ELSE
      advance-to-next-diagonal
  END;
```

and

```
DEFINE-NEW-INSTRUCTION zag-move AS
  BEGIN
    IF front-is-clear THEN
      zag-down-right
    ELSE
      advance-to-next-diagonal
  END;
```

The moving instructions **zig-move** and **zag-move** operate in a similar fashion; therefore, we discuss only **zig-move**. When Karel is able to keep zigging, the **zig-move** instruction moves it diagonally to the next corner; otherwise, the robot is blocked by the western boundary wall and must advance northward to the next diagonal. We now write the instruction that advances Karel to the next diagonal.

```
DEFINE-NEW-INSTRUCTION advance-to-next-diagonal AS
  BEGIN
    IF facing-west THEN
      turnright
    ELSE
      turnleft;
    move;
    turnaround
  END;
```

The **advance-to-next-diagonal** instruction starts by facing Karel away from the origin; it turns a different direction depending on whether the robot has been zigging or zagging. In either case, Karel then moves one corner farther away from the origin and turns around. If Karel has been zigging on the current diagonal, after executing `advance-to-next-diagonal`, the robot is positioned to continue by zagging on the next diagonal, and vice versa.

Observe that when Karel executes a `zig-left-up` or a `zag-down-right` instruction, it must visit two corners. The first is visited temporarily, and the second is catty-corner from Karel's starting corner. When thinking about these instructions, we should ignore the intermediate corner and just remember that these instructions move Karel diagonally. Also notice that the temporarily visited corner is guaranteed not to have a beeper on it, because it is part of the wave front that Karel visited while it was on the previous diagonal sweep.

Trace Karel's execution of `find-beeper` in the sample situation presented in Figure 6–2 to acquaint yourself with its operation; try to get a feel for how all these instructions fit together to accomplish the task. Pay particularly close attention to the `advance-to-next-diagonal` instruction. Test `find-beeper` in situations where the beeper is on the origin and next to either boundary wall.

6.3 DOING ARITHMETIC

In this section we describe how Karel can be given additional problems and how we can program the robot to compute sums. Suppose we want Karel to add the numbers 6 and 3. We can represent this problem in Karel's world by placing a beeper on the question corner of 6th Street and 3rd Avenue. Karel's answer to this problem is represented by putting down the beeper somewhere along 1st Street; the avenue that this beeper must be placed on is the sum of the two numbers being added. For this example, Karel should deposit the beeper on 1st Street and 9th Avenue. We call this the answer corner. In general, if the question corner is Sth Street and Ath Avenue, then the answer corner should be 1st Street and ($S + A$)th Avenue.

The addition problem can be partitioned into two separate phases. In the first phase, Karel must locate the question corner and pick up the beeper. This phase can be accomplished by executing a `find-beeper` instruction followed by a `pickbeeper` instruction. During the second phase, Karel computes the sum of the two numbers and then puts the beeper down on the answer corner. We can transcribe this plan into a program that solves the entire problem.

```
BEGINNING-OF-EXECUTION
    find-beeper;
    pickbeeper;
    compute-sum;
    putbeeper;
    turnoff
END-OF-EXECUTION
```

The sum can be computed by instructing Karel to zag down toward 1st Street. Before writing the **compute-sum** instruction, let's see why zagging helps to solve the problem. Assume that Karel has found the beeper on Sth Street and Ath Avenue. By performing a **zag-down-right** instruction, the robot moves to the corner of $(S - 1)$ street and $(A + 1)$ avenue. In our example, Karel moves from 6th Street and 3rd Avenue to 5th Street and 4th Avenue. This happens because the **zag-down-right** instruction decreases the street number that Karel is on by one (Karel moves south by one block) and increases the avenue number by one (Karel moves east by one block).

The invariant during **compute-sum** is that the sum of the street number and the avenue number of Karel's position is always $S + A$. (That is, the sum is always equal to Karel's original street number plus avenue number.) By executing a **zag-down-right** instruction, Karel preserves this invariant because of the following property of arithmetic:

$$S + A = (S - 1) + (A + 1)$$

If Karel continues performing **zag-down-right** instructions whenever its front is clear, the robot will repeatedly move south (and east) until it arrives at 1st Street. By continuing to subtract 1 from Karel's street number while adding 1 to Karel's avenue number, our invariant equation tells us that

$$S + A = (S - 1) + (A + 1) = (S - 2) + (A + 2) = \cdots = 1 + (A + S - 1)$$

Therefore, when Karel's street position decreases to 1, the avenue position will be $A + S - 1$. To complete the sum, all Karel must do is move one avenue to the east. The robot will then be on the answer corner of 1st Street and $(A + S)$th Avenue. Karel's complete motion for the proposed example is illustrated in Figure 6–3.

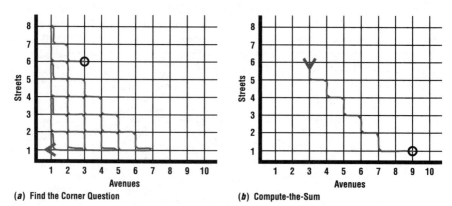

(*a*) Find the Corner Question   (*b*) Compute-the-Sum

Figure 6–3   Two Phases of Computing a Sum

The definition for the `compute-sum` instruction is as follows:

```
DEFINE-NEW-INSTRUCTION compute-sum AS
  BEGIN
    face-south;
    WHILE front-is-clear DO
      zag-down-right;
    face-east;
    move
  END;
```

Why have we included a `face-south` instruction immediately before the `WHILE` loop? We must do so because the specifications for the `find-beeper` instruction say nothing about which direction Karel is facing when `find-beeper` finishes. (In fact, sometimes Karel will be facing west, and sometimes Karel will be facing south when `find-beeper` finishes). To satisfy the directional precondition for `zag-down-right`, we must guarantee that Karel is facing south before executing the `WHILE` loop.

In general, programs that we write by using stepwise refinement are especially susceptible to bugs caused by unsatisfied preconditions. This type of error is initially very easy to overlook, so we must be careful and we must try to catch and correct unsatisfied precondition bugs as we develop our programs.

Along similar lines, what can we say about the `face-east` instruction? In this case, we know that Karel has been correctly zagging; therefore, the robot is guaranteed to be facing south immediately before executing the `face-east` instruction. Consequently, in this instance we can replace `face-east` by a `turnleft` instruction, but we do not advise performing this replacement. The `face-east` instruction is more descriptive than `turnleft`, and therefore we suggest that `compute-sum` remain in its present form.

6.4 PROBLEM SET

The following problems use the recursion, searching, and arithmetic methods discussed in this chapter. Some of the following problems use combinations of the `zig-left-up` and `zag-down-right` instructions, or simple variants of them. Each problem is difficult to solve, but once a plan is discovered (probably through an "aha experience"), the program that implements the solution will not be too difficult to write. In all these problems, you may assume that `find-beeper` has already been defined, so you are not required to write its definition in your programs. You may also assume that there are no wall sections in the world except for Problem 2. Finally, you should assume that Karel starts with no beepers in its beeper-bag, unless you are told otherwise. Do not make any assumptions about Karel's starting corner or starting direction, unless they are specified in the problem.

1. Rewrite your program that solves Problem 5.9–20 using a recursive instead of an iterative method.

2. Karel has graduated to advanced carpet layer. Karel must carpet the completely enclosed room. Only one beeper can be placed on each corner. The room may be any size and any shape. Figure 6–4 shows one possible floor plan. Karel is not to carpet the gray area. Karel may start from any place within the room and may be facing any direction.

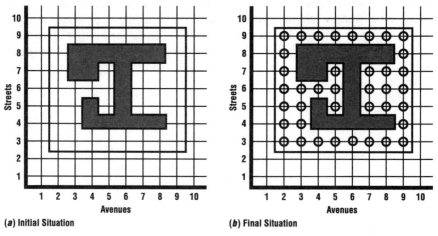

(a) Initial Situation   (b) Final Situation

Figure 6–4   A Big Carpeting Job

3. Rewrite both `zig-left-up` and `zag-down-right` so that they automatically satisfy their directional preconditions.

4. Assume that there is a beeper on 1st Street and *N*th Avenue. Program Karel to find it and move to *N*th Street and 1st Avenue.

5. Assume that there is a beeper on Sth Street and Ath Avenue, and that Karel has two beepers in its beeper-bag. Program Karel to put the beepers from its beeper-bag on to 1st Street and Ath Avenue and Sth Street and 1st Avenue. The original beeper must remain at the corner it starts on.

6. Assume that there is a beeper on 1st Street and Ath Avenue. Program Karel to double the avenue number; the robot must move this beeper to 1st Street and $2A$th Avenue. (For example, a beeper on 1st Street and 7th Avenue must be moved to 1st Street and 14th Avenue.) *Hint:* Use the west boundary wall as in Problem 6.4–4.

7. Assume that Karel starts its task with an infinite number of beepers in its beeper-bag. Also assume that there is a beeper on 1st Street and Nth Avenue. Program Karel to leave N beepers on the origin.

8. Assume that there is a beeper on Sth Street and 1st Avenue and a beeper on 1st Street and Ath Avenue. Program Karel to put one of these beepers on Sth Street and Ath Avenue. Karel must put the other beeper in its beeper-bag. *Hint:* There are many ways to plan this task. Here are two suggestions: (1) move one beeper south while moving the other beeper north; (2) continue moving one beeper until it is directly over (or to the right of) the stationary beeper. If done correctly, both methods will result in one beeper being placed on the answer corner.

9. Assume that Karel has a beeper in its beeper-bag and that there is another beeper on 1st Street and Ath Avenue. Program Karel to place one of the beepers on 1st Street and 2 to the Ath power Avenue. This expression is 2 raised to the Ath power or 1 doubled A times. For example, when A is 5, 2 to the Ath power is 32. *Hint:* This problem uses instructions similar to those used to solve Problem 6.4–6. Karel can use the second beeper to count the number of times it must double the number 1.

10. Repeat Problem 6.4–9, but this time the answer corner is 1st Street and 3 to the Ath power Avenue. Try to reuse as much of the previous program as possible.

11. Program Karel to place beepers in an outward spiral until its beeper-bag is empty. Assume that Karel will run out of beepers before it is stopped by the boundary walls. One example is shown in Figure 6–5.

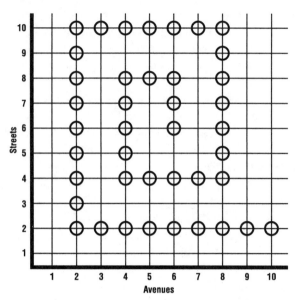

Figure 6–5   A Spiral

12. Assume that Karel has two beepers and that there is another beeper on Sth Street and Ath Avenue. Program Karel to deposit one of these beepers on the corner of 1st Street and SAth Avenue. (This expression is S multiplied by A.)

13. Assume that Karel has three beepers in its beeper-bag and that there is another beeper on Sth Street and Ath Avenue. Program Karel to deposit a beeper on the corner of 1st Street and S to the Ath power Avenue. (This expression is S raised to the power of A.)

14. Assume that Karel has three beepers in its beeper-bag and that there is another beeper on Sth Street and Ath Avenue. Program Karel to put a beeper on the corner of 1st Street and GCD(S,A)th Ave. The GCD of two numbers is their Greatest Common Divisor. For example, the GCD of 6 and 15 is 3. *Hint:* Use Euclid's subtractive method.

15. Assume that Karel has N beepers in its beeper-bag. Program the robot to place beepers on 1st Street and all avenues that represent prime numbers between 1st Avenue and (N − SquareRoot of N)th Avenue.

16. If you enjoy computer science and eventually take a course in computability theory, fondly recall the days you spent programming Karel and try to solve the following problem: Prove that Karel, even without the aid of any beepers, is equivalent to a Turing machine. *Hint:* Use the equivalence between Turing machines and 2-counter automata. Remember that Karel's instructions are not mutually recursive, so state information must be encoded in some other manner.

ROBOT PROGRAMMING SUMMARY

PRIMITIVE INSTRUCTIONS

1) move	Karel moves one block forward.
2) turnleft	Karel pivots 90° to the left.
3) pickbeeper	Karel puts a beeper in its beeper-bag.
4) putbeeper	Karel places a beeper on the corner.
5) turnoff	Karel turns itself off.

BLOCK STRUCTURING INSTRUCTION

6) **BEGIN**
    <instruction>;
    <instruction>;
      .   .
      .   .
      .   .
    <instruction>;
    <instruction>
   END

CONDITIONAL INSTRUCTIONS

7) **IF** <test>
     THEN <instruction>
8) **IF** <test>
     THEN <instruction>
     ELSE <instruction>

REPETITION INSTRUCTIONS

9) **ITERATE** <positive-number> **TIMES**
     <instruction>

10) WHILE <test> DO
    <instruction>

THE MECHANISM FOR DEFINING NEW INSTRUCTIONS

11) DEFINE-NEW-INSTRUCTION <new-name> AS
    <instruction>

SPECIFYING A COMPLETE PROGRAM

12) BEGINNING-OF-PROGRAM

    DEFINE-NEW-INSTRUCTION <new-name> AS
    <instruction>;
        .
        .
        .
    DEFINE-NEW-INSTRUCTION <new-name> AS
    <instruction>;

    BEGINNING-OF-EXECUTION
      <instruction>;
        .   .
        .   .
        .   .
      <instruction>
    END-OF-EXECUTION
    END-OF-PROGRAM

BRACKETED WORDS

1) <instruction>   Any of the robot instructions (1–10)
2) <new-name>   Any new word (in lower-case letters, numbers, "-")
3) <positive-number> Any positive number
4) <test>   Any of the following:
                      front-is-clear, front-is-blocked,
                      left-is-clear, left-is-blocked,
                      right-is-clear, right-is-blocked,
                      next-to-a-beeper, not-next-to-a-beeper,
                      facing-north, not-facing-north,
                      facing-south, not-facing-south,
                      facing-east, not-facing-east,
                      facing-west, not-facing-west,
                      any-beepers-in-beeper-bag,
                      no-beepers-in-beeper-bag

TECHNICAL TERM INDEX

INSTRUCTION INDEX

Instructions that occur in the text are listed in this index. The page number refers to the page where the instruction is first defined. If an instruction has been defined several times, additional page numbers are provided for the subsequent definitions only if they differ substantially from the original definition.